SONIC
VISUALS FOR MUSIC

COMPILED & EDITED BY ROBERT KLANTEN, HENDRIK HELLIGE, TOM HULAN

Dietmar Dath

Dreaming the synaesthetic country

Here's the high-altitude map for you.

This country, connecting soundscapes via a visibly countable sum of all their imaginable histories, is a quilt. There is no navel here, no axis mundi, but it's not exactly de-centralized either. What you're dealing with is an area made up of cells. Pull back far enough and you can see it glimmer; get closer and you will be able to identify individual units. Now you're getting somewhere. Your new frame of reference, to be defied at the inhabitants' own peril, is the perfect square. We'll get to flyers, posters and other rectangles later and in a more implicit fashion.

But concentrate on the square for a moment. Within its boundaries, you're pretty much on your own. Shapes may look pretty constructivist at times (that's what we call minimalism 'round these parts). Colour, like virtue, is its own reward, though, when taking the scenic route on the ground level, you might feel that especially the magenta and pink hues that mushroom in some of the more acidic neighbourhoods might make you feel as if you're travelling along the laser beam inside a CD player, "speeding along through an unfathomable void toward some sort of crystalline creature glowing with a myriad of colours, which turn out to be the eternally elusive maximal dualistic unity" (Stanislaw Witkiewicz) of binary coding which underlies both the pixels and the smallest units of sound. Do you perhaps wish to contribute to this massive piece of land art of the mind? By all means, go ahead. You may try your luck with a gouache or an engraving. You may draw nervous squiggles on an egg-shell-white background. You might fill your imaginary realm with an embryonic drawing like the one Walter Benjamin came up with when under the influence of mescaline in 1934.

You might draw aliens with eyes that really are the windows to souls accustomed to pondering the imponderable, or you may highlight a grainy portrait of a stubborn child. You might show your audience sexy, pouting, sleepy girls – that can never hurt – or angelic, frowning, leather-clad boys – always a wise choice as well. You might invite the public to identify with robots and skeletons. You can get as heraldic, numismatic or iconographic as you damn well please. You could also do collages, frottages or assemblages that would shame Max Ernst. If that does not strike your fancy, you might cover your CD in cardboard, in paper, in cheap leatherette.

You may also, if it pleases you, cover it in feathers, as if inside there were chickens hatching, not sounds. Go pop, op, neo-geo, lettrist or surrealist, go easy, go it alone, make it shiny and slick or crude and coarse, but make it new. If the audience asks "what is this?", you will have succeeded.

In order to achieve this, you should leave it open whether your covers are intended for anthropologic, psychologic, mineralogic or paleontologic demonstration.

Show new people such as have never been seen before, if you please.

You might give your intended viewers a stark, black outline of the artist or artists featured, metaphysically backlit by the viewer's suspicion that you did something to a photograph to achieve this effect, whereas, in reality, it was all drawn with your mouse and then reduced, refined and reworked until it fit.

You may go for any and all kinds of illusionist tricks and techniques of verisimilitude – a two-dimensional surface like the one you're facing now can be made to look like vacuum-formed plastic or a tin license plate, like industrial enamel on canvas, like lead and steel, like acrylic on wood, like rusty plates of unknown metal, like an offset lithograph, like a computer screen, like a Polaroid shot, like a piece of forensic evidence, like a coloured plate from a particle detector, like murky photo-embedments in plastic or even – every punk rocker's perennial favourite – like shit.

Do you want to do a movie poster for a one-show event? What's it going to be, Bergman or Spielberg, Godard or Kubrick, Blaxploitation cinema or art-house obscurity? Go for it. See where it leads you. Don't worry about genre – it's become increasingly difficult to judge whether a given icon of commercial art is aimed at the tastes of Hip-Hoppers or Heavy Metal maniacs.

This is the age of the skull and crossbones, the hammer and the bolt of lightning, the fist and the wheel freed from their former allegiance to the code of behaviour for sigla and systems for classifying any coat-of-arms you may catch a glance of in passing. We have entered a world where the detailed rendering of moods counts for more than mere tribal legibility.

Maybe you could play industrial effects against organic ones, make them bleed into each other, feed off one another. Go into those neon depths with small or large burdens of information, remember where the urban public lives. Think of your CD cover not as a painting to be hung on some blank wall, but as a piece of very small-scale architecture that has to fit in with a world where "central columns, sheathed in green ceramic, support a ceiling pocked with dust-furred ventilators, smoke detectors, speakers. Behind the columns, against the far wall, derelict shipping cartons huddle in a ragged train, improvised shelters constructed by the city's homeless." (William Gibson).

Use the green ceramic, use the shipping cartons, use the rags. Do you want to miniaturize marquee art? Do you like sewing or knitting? Have you ever smashed a pumpkin or shredded a flag? By all means, knock yourself out. However, there are still a number of things you may not do. You're not allowed to more than hint at the shameful glory of airbrushed double-LP covers from the seventies. Not just for reasons of constraint of space – we're talking mostly flyers and CD covers here; vinyl covers and the occasional boxed set are the fretful exception – but for the obvious reason that too much self-indulgence at the purely painterly level, too much artisanship in pursuit of a sight gag, can easily be misconstrued as the ill-conceived desire to tread the more unsavoury waters of easy parody and facile appropriation. If you want your stuff to convince anyone these days, please don't try to make them chuckle. They may do so at first, but they're going to hate you for it if the thing you made will stick around for a while, i.e. if the record is to be in frequent use. Also, please don't make too much of a fuss about the traces of your digital craft.

That was fine a decade ago, but now it tends to look like... well, have you ever seen dogs marking their territory the way dogs tend to do that? Avoid these things. They're just crass. The result looks like spoor, it's arrgghhh, it's ugh, and not nice in the sense of being gutsy or challenging.

Do not believe the lie that technology makes things bland and uniform, that it is responsible for the daily tedium and ennui of living through the ninety percent of popular culture, visual and otherwise, which seems to be sanitized and homogenized to the point of nausea. It's the commodity form that counts, not the tools. Technology does not necessarily eliminate freedom or "the subject." You can still be an author, you can still behave classically – even if it takes more to do so now than during the heyday of modernism, for reasons that have nothing to do with computers and everything with society. People create constraints and boundaries, not machines, and our myths still reflect that. "The maximum compact disc playing time (strictly according to legend) was determined after Philips consulted conductor Herbert von Karajan. He advised them that a disc should be able to hold his performance of the Beethoven Ninth Symphony without interruption." (Ken C. Pohlmann)

4

So forget "forgetting the author," forget white-label creativity or corporate anonymity, and while you're at it, beware of another highly charged ideological trap – the idea that the very notion of "skill" has migrated into the machines or, at the very least, into the varying dimensions of their handling by the artists in musical as well as in visual terms. This is a deeply misleading notion. For although the kind of admiration that computer-assisted work may fetch is not the same as that used to reward a big range of voice, fingers that can pick guitar strings at impressive speed or superior draughtsmanship, you're not so much going to be praised for specializing yourself out of existence, but rather for being able to integrate the divergent aspects of your work. If you get this right, you've already won.

The reason for this increased exchange value of integrational skill has a lot to do with what popular culture as a whole has wrought in the realm of commercial and not-so-commercial art during the last fifty years. It also has to do with the way this larger history has been repeated, in faster and almost superheated ways, since the advent of computer aided design and manufacturing of cultural artefacts about ten to fifteen years ago. Music was always at the forefront of this, or maybe it is more accurate to reverse this statement. At the forefront of this, even when the thing that was being changed was movies, television, sports or nightlife, there was always music.

For one of the most important features of pop music, even in its more outré or avant-garde modes, is that there's more to the music than just the music itself. Pop music is a social practise concerned with emphatic modes of appreciating things, moods and situations. And an "emphatic mode of appreciation" is, of course, something you can observe, you can see, something quintessentially visual. Posters, flyers and covers are not auxiliary stuff, not something on the side; they're part of the main event. Children, as the principle of stern education prescribes, should be seen and not heard. The austerity of classically occidental forms of music demands that they be heard and not seen, but pop music wants to be heard, seen and, if at all possible, even tasted. The responsibility faced by those who create the look of these things – whether a video, a CD cover or a flyer – is thus necessarily quite a large one. They're co-creators of content in a nontrivial sense, just as the garish colours of American pulp magazine covers did more then accentuate content. They rather defined what certain popular genres such as the thriller, the horror story or science-fiction were supposed to be, and to be about.

The pictures in this book are thumbnails of a synaesthetic way of life. They refer to the fact that seeing, hearing and tasting are meant to be interchangeable variants of emphatically informational experience. The role of the computer in this is that it allows the integration of the different spices for the different soul foods of the senses. Even as early as on the level of pre-production you can plan your CD tracks on the same machine that you're going to use for designing the record's cover, for animating, cutting and/or editing the video, for creating the poster or constructing the website that announces the project, for sending out the mails that announce the record's impending release. And don't forget that your target audience may also download anything you create on similar machines.

Far from being the only one, this constitutes at least the most important reason for popular culture's extreme eagerness in welcoming the third industrial revolution, with which it has come to identify itself so readily and completely that it seems at times as if all popular culture and music before the computer and the Net were just test stages, rehearsals, embodiments avant la lettre of electronic culture. The synaesthetic public that the pictures assembled in this book addresses thus gives a social and practical answer to the old riddle baffling sensualist philosophers from the early day of the Age of Enlightenment: can blind people see in their dreams?

The proper neurophysiological answer to this depends, of course, on whether the blindness dates from the person's birth or was acquired in later life. If you're born blind, the visual cortex has never been "gauged" to perception; there is no inductive knowledge of visual space. Therefore, you do not "see" anything in dreams, although you might experience other hallucinatory adventures, say, in acoustic and/or tactile space.

But if your eyes have ever been open at all, close them before looking for your inner CD cover. Wait for the brain to speak in tongues and be assured that the many voices you will be hearing, though scary, are friendly.

Here's what they will say to start the conversation:

we have such sights to show you.

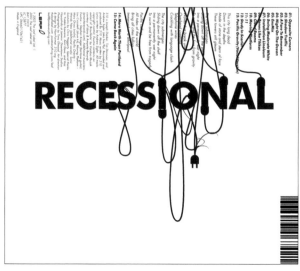

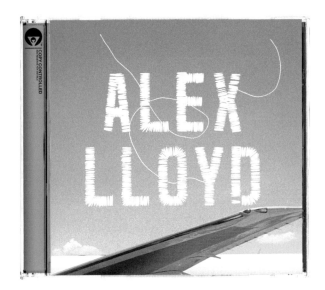

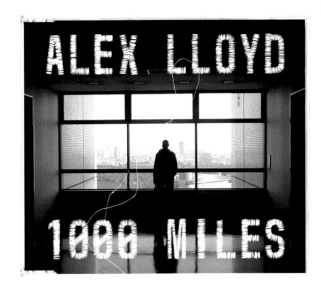

Design   NonFormat
Music   Alex Lloyd
Format   CD Covers

7

simian
chemistry is what we are
(lp)

fig 1: st bernhard

simian
mr. crow
(ep)

simian
one dimension
(ep)

simian
the wisp
(ep)

Design   Big Active
Music   Simian
Format   CD Covers

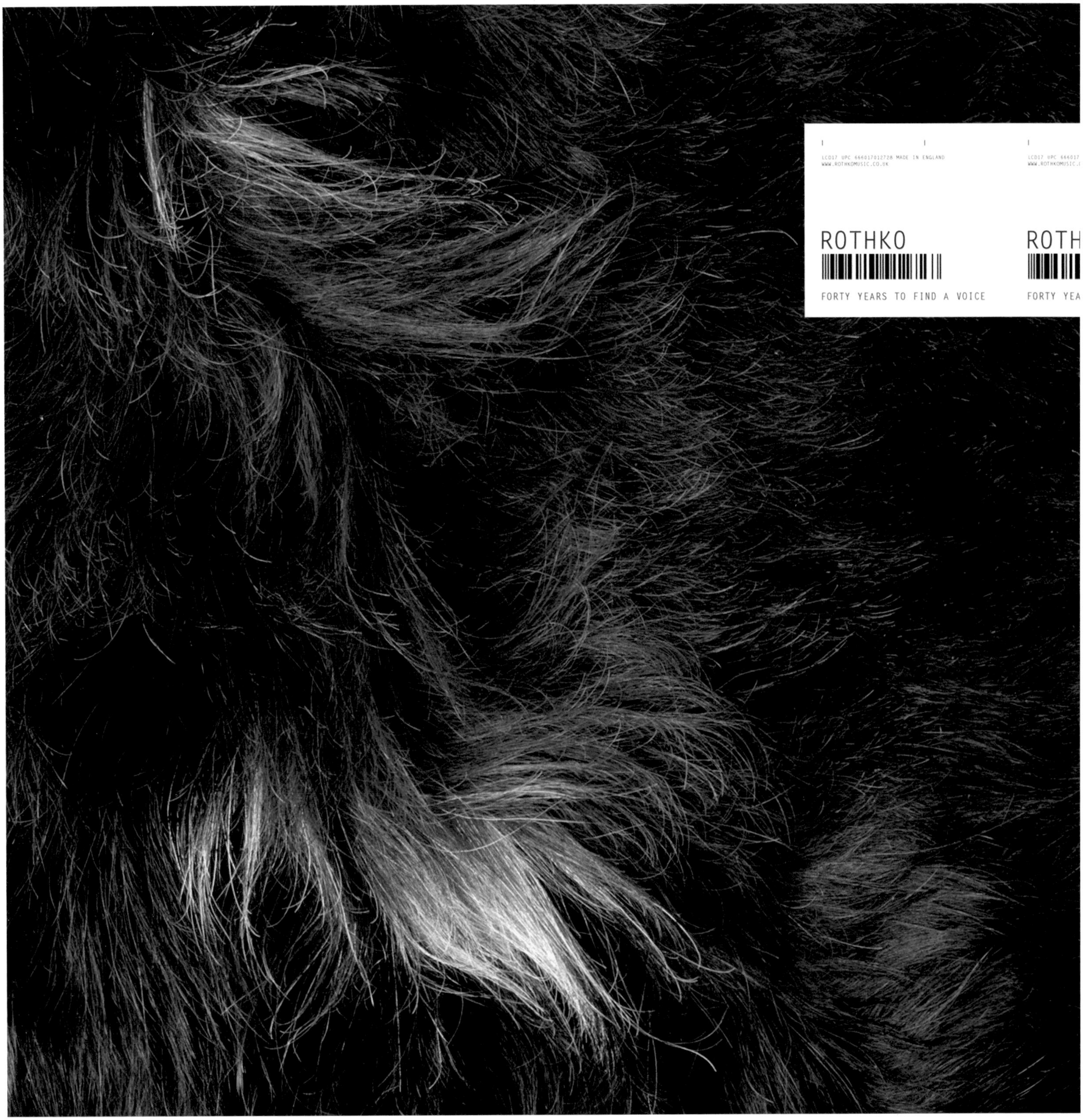
LCD17 UPC 666017012728 MADE IN ENGLAND
WWW.ROTHKOMUSIC.CO.UK
ROTHKO
FORTY YEARS TO FIND A VOICE

Design NonFormat
Music Rothko
Format Vinyl Sleeve

Goldfrapp

STRICT MACHINE

Design   Big Active
Music   Goldfrapp
Format   CD Covers

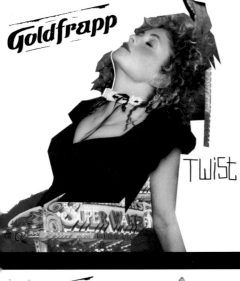

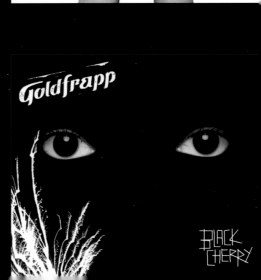

Design   Sarah Littasy
Music   Tosca
Format   CD Covers, Vinyl Sleeves

Design	!K7	Marc Schilkowski
Music	Peace Orchestra	Kruder & Dorfmeister
Format	CD Covers	CD Covers

DIE TOTEN HOSEN REICH &
SEXY II DIE FETTEN JAHRE / IHRE ALLERGRÖSSTEN ERFOLGE

DIE TOTEN HOSEN REICH & SEXY II
DIE FETTEN JAHRE / IHRE ALLERGRÖSSTEN ERFOLGE / JKP 57 / 5245-08978-2

Design   Dirk Rudolph
Music   Die Toten Hosen
Format   CD Cover, Book

14

CD1 01 PUSHED AGAIN / 02 BONNIE & CLYDE / 03 SCHÖN SEIN / 04 FRAUEN DIESER WELT / 05 PARADIES / 06 NICHTS BLEIBT FÜR DIE EWIGKEIT / 07 WAS ZÄHLT / 08 UNSTERBLICH / 09 IRRE / 10 STEH AUF, WENN DU AM BODEN BIST / 11 WARUM WERDE ICH NICHT SATT? / 12 MADELAINE (AUS LÜDENSCHEID) / 13 WEIHNACHTSMANN VOM DACH / 14 ZUR HÖLLE UND ZURÜCK / 15 NUR ZU BESUCH / 16 NIEMALS EINER MEINUNG / 17 BAYERN / 18 AULD LANG SYNE / 19 ZEHN KLEINE JÄGERMEISTER / 20 SCHÖNEN GRUSS, AUF WIEDERSEH'N / GESAMT 75:45

CD2 01 ENTENHAUSEN BLEIBT STABIL / 02 HANG ON SLOOPY / 03 VOR DEM STURM / 04 WAHRE LIEBE / 05 ABITUR / 06 DIE „7" IST ALLES / 07 TOUT POUR SAUVER L'AMOUR / 08 REST DER WELT / 09 POLICE ON MY BACK / 10 KLEINER JUNGE / 11 IN GOTTES NAMEN / 12 ALKOHOL / 13 LONG WAY FROM LIVERPOOL / 14 EIN WITZ / 15 BABYLON'S BURNING / 16 ALLES IST EINS / 17 GEH AUS DEM WEG / 18 100 TAGE BIS ZUM UNTERGANG / 19 WALTER NOVEMBER – EIN INTERVIEW / 20 YOU'LL NEVER WALK ALONE / GESAMT 62:37

6 52450 89782 4

Design   Yacht Associates
Music   MJ Cool
Format   CD Covers

Design   Zip
Music   Space Cowboy
Format   CD Cover

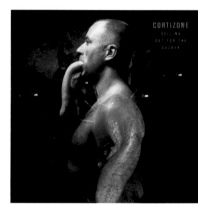

Design   Dirk Rudolph
Music   Cortizone
Format   CD Cover, Booklet

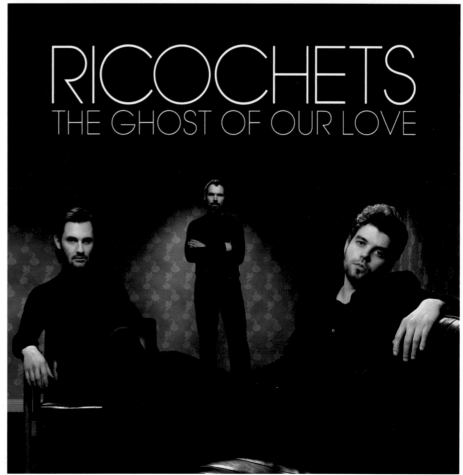

Design   Sarah Littasy   Martin Kvamme
Music   Tosca   Ricochets
Format   CD Cover   CD Cover, Booklet

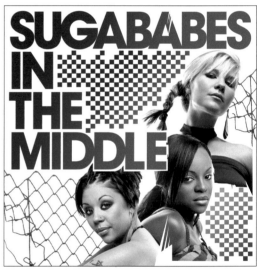

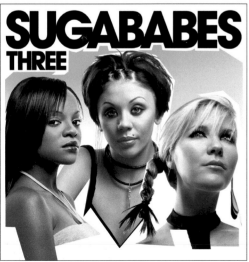

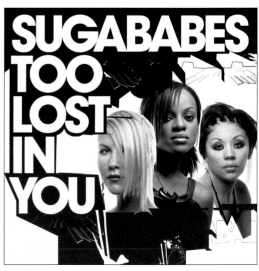

Design   Positron   Big Active
Music   AI   Sugarbabes
Format   CD Cover   CD Covers

Design   Zip
Music   So Solid Crew
Format   CD Cover

The Aim Of Design Is To Define Space

GÖTZ ALSMANN

17 NEUE SPANNENDE ABENTEUER

Lieder über ferne Länder... verwunschene Oasen...
okkulte Riten... geheimnisvolle Frauen...

TABU!

BOUTIQUE VERLAG   HEFT NR.1

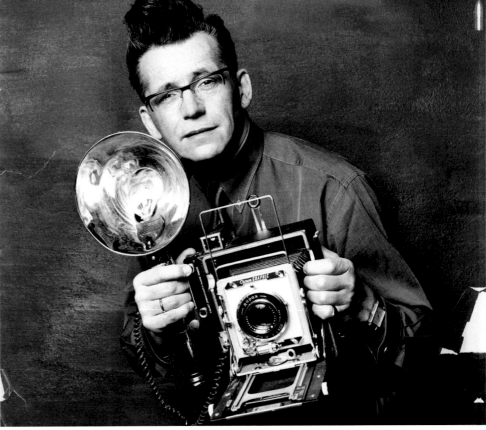

01
Nana
(CASSERES)
verlegt bei Globe-Music
3:17

02
Weit weg von hier
(GÖTZ/BRADTKE) EDITION RIALTO 3:37

03
DU BIST SO LIEB ZU MIR
(MEYER/SCHULZ-GELLEN)
Albert Bennefeld Musikverlag
3:29

04
EIN KLEINER BÄR MIT GROSSEN OHREN
(Halletz)
Hermann Schneider Verlags KG 2:40

05
ES WAR EIN MÄDCHEN UND EIN MATROSE
Text und Musik von Grothe/Dehmel
im Verlag von **Beboton** 2:15

06
ICH FAND EIN HERZ IN PORTOFINO
(Buscaglione/Chiosso/Marchesi)
EDITION REVERE
3:09

07
BRAUCHST DU FÜR'S HERZ 'NE MISS?
Duett mit
Jasmin Tabatabai
(Jary/Balz) Michael Jary Produktion 3:37

08
Küss mich, tatarisches Mädchen!
(Alsmann) Roof Music 3:15

09
Fräulein Mabel
(Erhardt)
Edition Simon Musikverlag KG
2:09

10
DER SCHLANGEN-BESCHWÖRER
(Weiss/Schwenn/Pfötzschner)
ARCADIA VERLAG GMBH
3:17

11
KOMMST DU MIT AUF EINEN
Mokka?
(HALLETZ/WERNER) Verlag:
Michael Jary Produktion
2:47

07/12
TABU!
(LECUONA/SCHWENN)
SOUTHERN MUS. PUB. CO. LTD.
6:50

13
MAMBO DE LA FÉE DRAGÉE
TSCHAIKOWSKY/ALSMANN
ROOF MUSIC
2:03

14
D·O·M·I·N·O
(Ferrari/Plante) Verlag:
ARPEGE EDITIONS MUSICALES
3:19

15
DAS WÄR' WAS
(Eine Freundin so goldig wie du)
(Meisel/Rosen/Lion)
MEISEL MUSIKVERLAG 3:21

16
Karawanen-Song
(Caravan)
(Ellington/Tizol/Siegel)
R.M. Siegel-Musikedition
4:40

17
Abschiedslied
(Erhardt) Manuskript
2:25

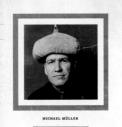

Design   Dirk Rudolph
Music   Götz Alsmann
Format   CD Cover

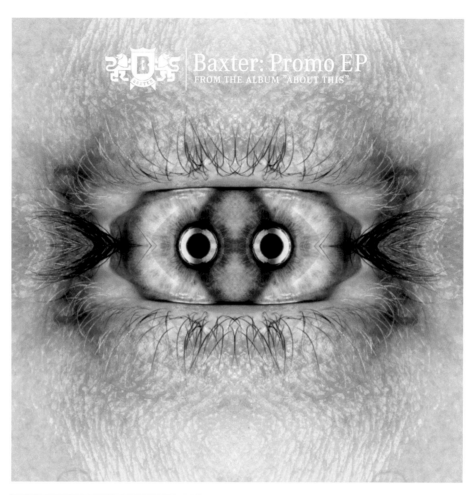

Baxter: Promo EP
FROM THE ALBUM "ABOUT THIS"

About This
Baxter

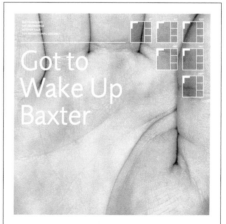

Got to
Wake Up
Baxter

Design   Zion
Music   Baxter
Format   CD Covers

GRAND TONE MUSIC

Design	Fellow Designers
Music	Grand Tone Music
Format	CD Cover

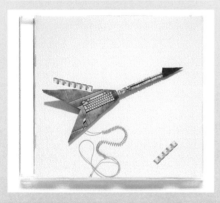

CONSOLE
→ RESET THE RESET

Design   Faktor
Music   Konsole
Format   CD Cover

28

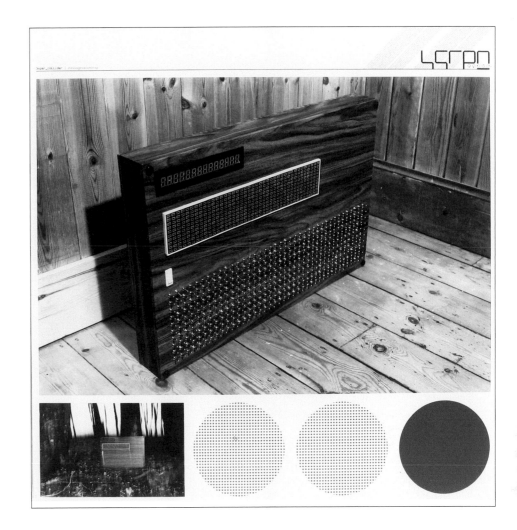

Design   Red
Music   Super Collider
Format   CD Cover

Design	Brainbox	Faktor
Music	The Music Effect	Jasmin Tabatabei
Format	CD Cover	CD Cover

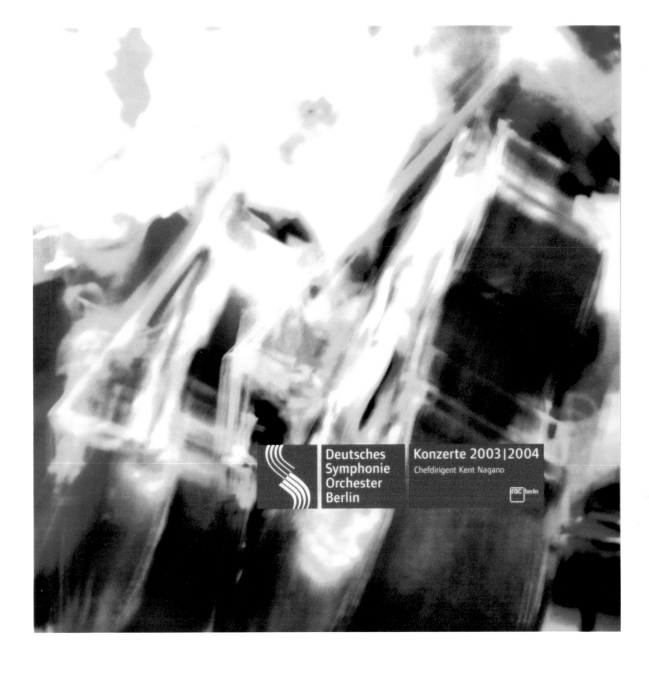

Deutsches
Symphonie
Orchester
Berlin

Konzerte 2003|2004
Chefdirigent Kent Nagano

roc berlin

Design   Faktor
Music   DSO Berlin
Format   CD Cover

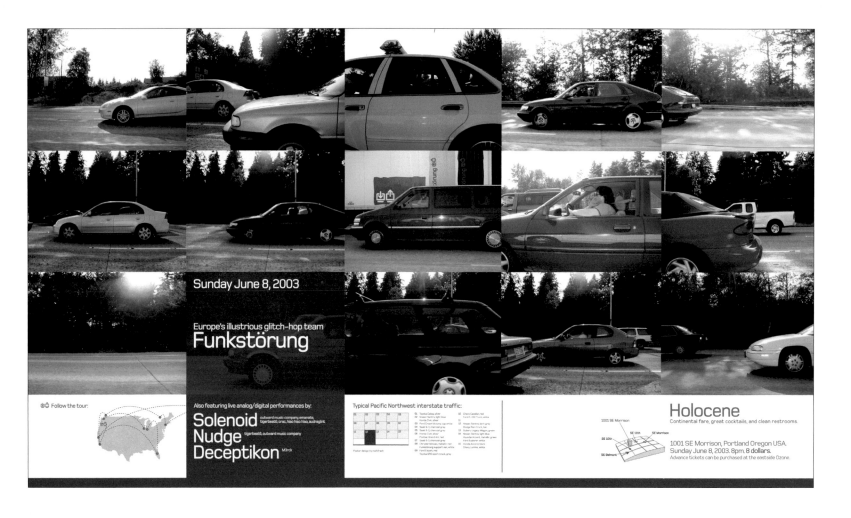

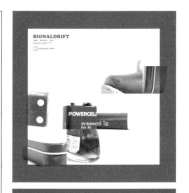

Design   mFresh
Music   Various
Format   Poster, Flyer, CD Cover

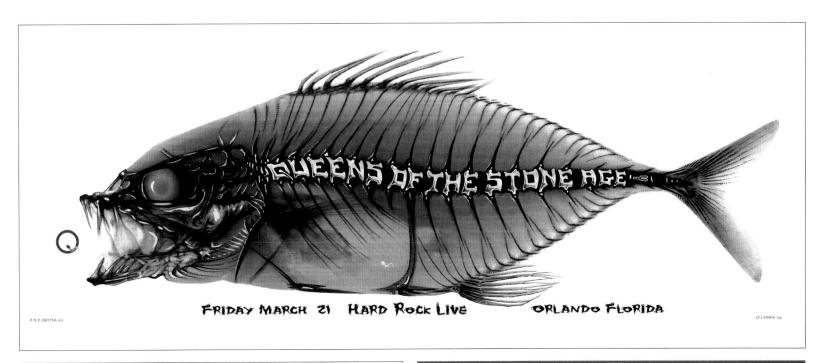

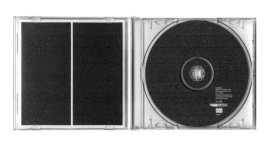

Design	Emek	Carlos Segura	KarlssonWilker
Music	Queens of the Stoneage	Lesley Spencer	Sideshow
Format	Gig Poster	CD Cover	CD Cover

33

Liam Gillick
meets
Scott Olson
in Japan

Joseph Suchy
Canoeing Instructional

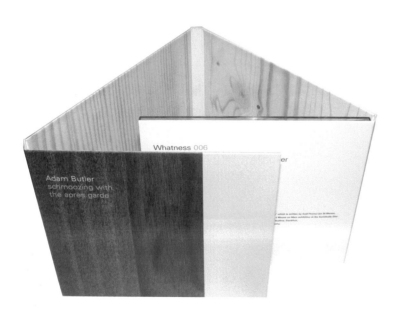

Adam Butler
schmoozing with
the après garde

Design   Surface
Music   Various
Format   CD Covers

Ekkehard Ehlers
Sebastian Meissner
Thom Willelms
Music for
William Forsythe

Ekkehard Ehlers
Sebastian Meissner
Thom Willems
Music for
William Forsythe

Sebastian Meissner

Ekkehard Ehlers 2001

Ekkehard Ehlers 2001

Willems 2002

Marc Ushmi meets Reverend Galloway
on Ernst Busch

eit, vorwärts die Zeit.
y plate? Die Solidaritate.
rmers hold em up

Marc Ushmi meets Reverend Galloway
on Ernst Busch

inuten kommt es immer an.
n Kinderspiel aus Glas.
verschwunden.

chende Zwings,
en ist es nur im Traum

Aerial Riverseries
Frank Bretschneider
on Olafur Eliasson

Aerial Riverseries
Frank Bretschneider
on Olafur Eliasson

elieve, a matter of cultivation. As much as
vith memory and recognition, our relation
s closely derived from our cultural habitat.
t thirty for various whites. Lime has a
mes thrown into mass graves to prevent
s hospitals used the lime to whitewash
olor white was equal to clean. Many of the
clean space – or composition – was the
elf-realisation. Imagine if lime by nature
ow well-known white cube museum would

Design   NonFormat   Zion
Music   Asa Chang, Jun Ray   Perfect Match
Format   CD Packagings   CD Packaging

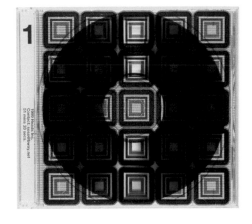

Design	Shrine	So Takahashi
Music	Synesthesia	Heads
Format	CD Packaging	CD Packaging

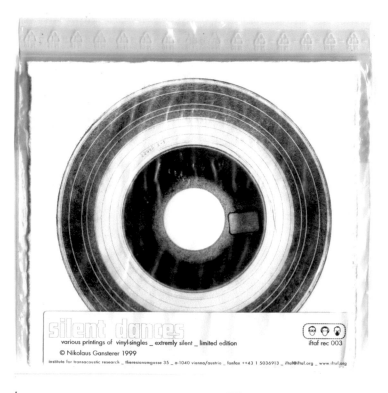

silent dances
various printings of vinyl-singles _ extremly silent _ limited edition
© Nikolaus Gansterer 1999
institute for transacoustic research _ theresianumgasse 35 _ a-1040 vienna/austria _ fonfax ++43 1 5036913 _ iftaf@iftaf.org _ www.iftaf.org

iftaf rec 003

Design   Transaccoustic Research
Music   Silent Dances
Format   CD Packaging

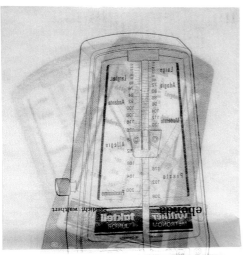

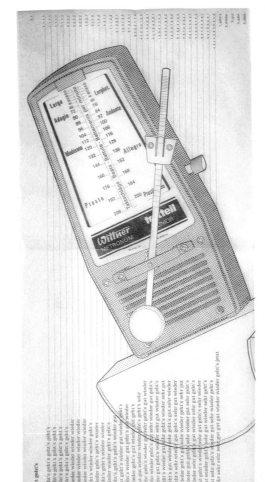

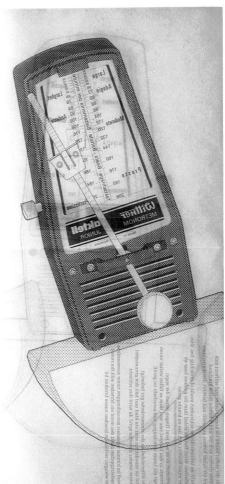

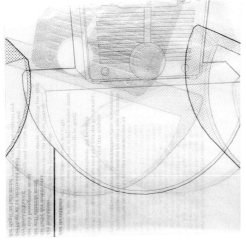

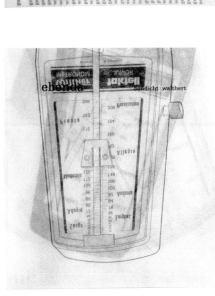

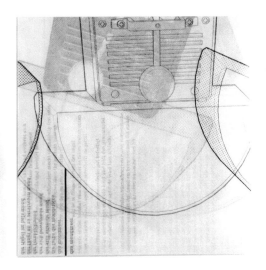

Design   Martin Woodtli
Music   Ebenda
Format   CD Packaging

FUNKSTÖRUNG. VICEVERSA. CD

FEATURING REWORKS VOR PLAID.JAY-JAY JOHANSON.NILS
PETTER MOLVAER.A GUY CALLED GERALD.BEANS.SPEEDY J.
IKE YARD.THE NOTWIST.FUNCKARMA. PHILLIP BOA + THE
VOODOOCLUB.TOCOTRONIC.JEAN MICHEL JARRE

7 30003 71082 7

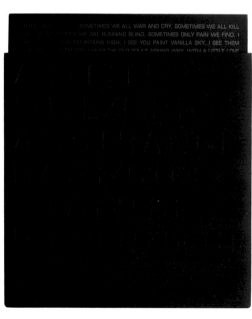

Design   K7   Big Active
Music   Funkstörung   Syntax
Format   CD Packaging   CD Packaging

40

KREIDLER | MORT AUX VACHES

THIS IS A LIMITED EDITION   722 /1000

TIN FOIL
STAR

VPRO

MORT AUX VACHES

RYOJI IKEDA
MORT AUX VACHES
1 HEADPHONICS [VPRO VERSION] :: +/– [VPRO VERSION]
2 LSDS
PRODUCED AND PERFORMED BY RYOJI IKEDA. RECORDED
APRIL 15, 1998. COMMISSIONED BY VPRO RADIO 5 "DE
AVONDEN". THANKS > GEERTJE KAMER AND JAN HIDDINK >
STAALPLAAT, P.O. BOX 11453, 1001 GL AMSTERDAM, THE
NETHERLANDS, P.O. BOX 83296, PORTLAND, OR 97293, USA.
SLEEVE BY ALORENZ, BERLIN. THIS IS A LIMITED EDITION.
YOUR NUMBER: /1000

Design   A.Lorenz
Music   Mort Aux Vaches Series
Format   CD Packaging

Design   Airside
Music   Various
Format   CD / Vinyl Packagings

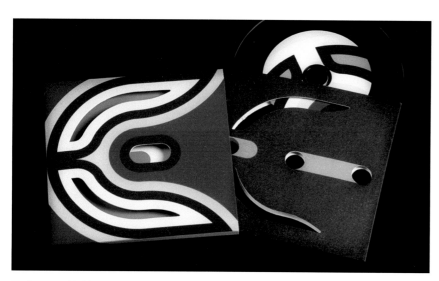

Design   Airside
Music   Various
Format   CD / Vinyl Packagings

Design   Insect   So Takahashi
Music   Jack Planck   Various
Format   Vinyl Packaging   CD / Vinyl Packagings

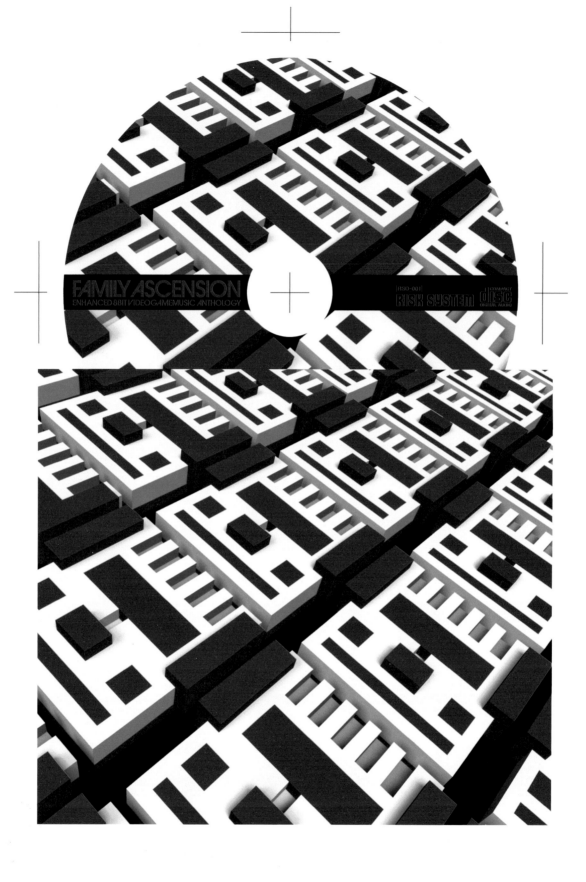

FAMILY ASCENSION
ENHANCED 8BIT VIDEOGAMEMUSIC ANTHOLOGY

[RSD-001]
RISK SYSTEM
COMPACT
disc
DIGITAL AUDIO

Design   Quentaro "ANI" Fujimoto
Music   Family Ascension - Enhanced 8bit Videogamemusic Anthology
Format   CD Packaging

46

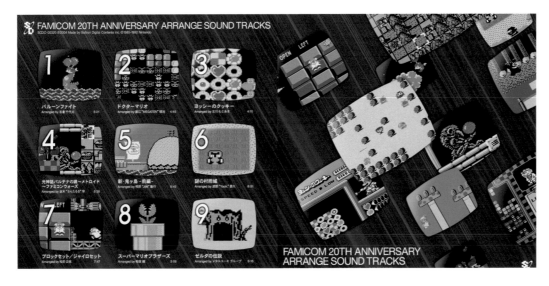

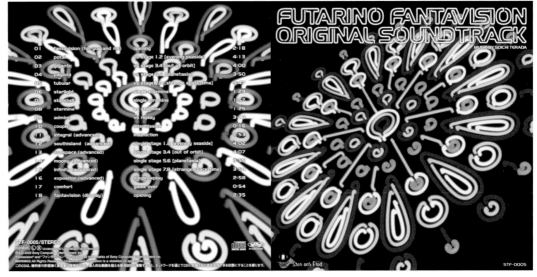

Design   Quentaro "ANI" Fujimoto
Music   Various - Videogame Music
Format   CD Covers

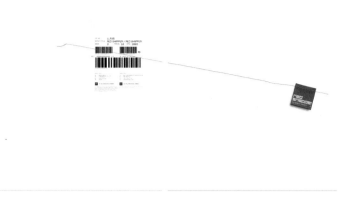

Design   NonFormat
Music   Red Snapper
Format   CD Cover

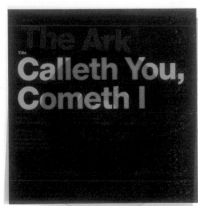

Design   Zion
Music   The Ark
Format   CD Cover

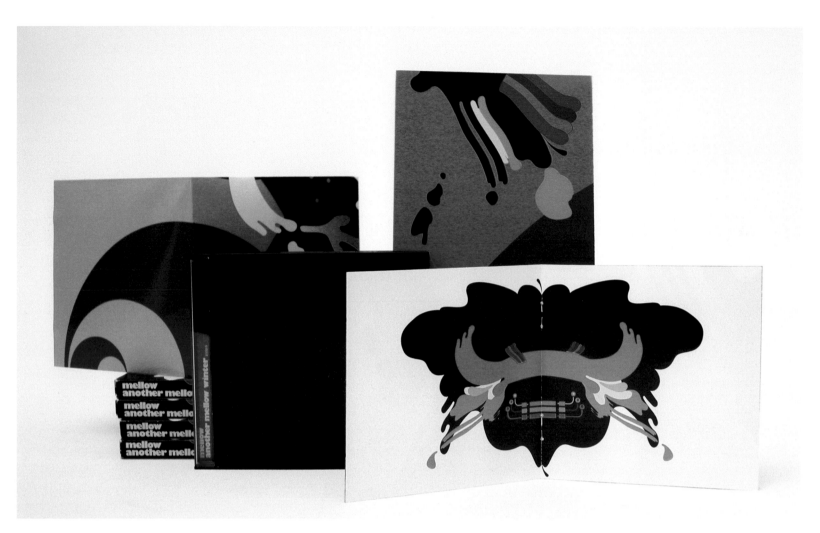

Design   Laurent Fetis
Music   Various
Format   CD Covers

50

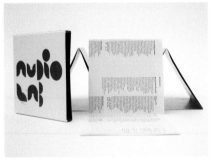

Design   Stylorouge   John Wiese
Music   Pretenders, Cerys Matthews, Show of Hands   Man is the Bastard Noise
Format   CD Covers   CD Cover

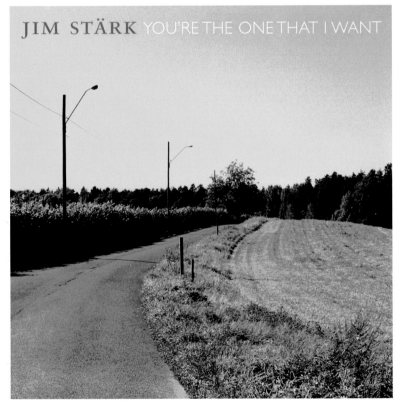

Design   Red   Rune Mortensen
Music   Meteorites   Jim Stärk
Format   Vinyl Sleeve CD Cover

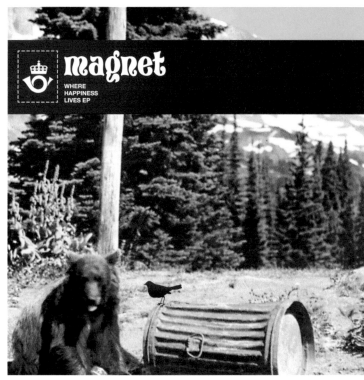

WHERE HAPPINESS LIVES /01
I'LL COME ALONG /02
HEAVIEST HEART /03
NOTHING HURTS NOW /04

www.HomeOfMagnet.com
FOR PROMOTIONAL USE ONLY

UD ULTIMATE DILEMMA

magnet
WHERE
HAPPINESS
LIVES EP

WHERE HAPPINESS LIVES /01
I'LL COME ALONG /02
HEAVIEST HEART /03
NOTHING HURTS NOW /04

All tracks written by Magnet
Copyright control
Tracks 1 & 4 Produced by Magnet
Tracks 2 & 3 Produced by Magnet and Sir Dupemann
Recorded and mixed at Magnetophonic Labs / Bergen / Norway
Except Track 2 / mixed at Dupa / Bergen / Norway
Mastered by Chris Blair at Abbey Road / London
Additional musicians:
Kjell Specter / Stig Pluto / David Aasheim / Gullet
Artwork: Martin Kvamme
Management: James Sandom at SuperVision

www.HomeOfMagnet.com

All rights of the producer and owner of this recorded work
reserved. Unauthorised copying, public performance,
broadcasting, hiring or rental of this recording prohibited.

℗ & © 2002 Ultimate Dilemma
Distribution by 3MV/Pinnacle
+44 (0) 20 7378 8866
Made in England
www.ultimate-dilemma.com

magnet
WHERE
HAPPINESS
LIVES EP

Design   Martin Kvamme
Music   Magnet
Format   CD Covers

WHERE HAPPINESS LIVES /01
I'LL COME ALONG /02
HEAVIEST HEART /03
NOTHING HURTS NOW /04

UDRCDS048
www.HomeOfMagnet.com

All tracks written by Magnet
Copyright control
Tracks 1 & 4 Produced by Magnet
Tracks 2 & 3 Produced by Magnet and Sir Dupermann
Recorded and mixed at Magnetophonic Labs / Bergen / Norway
Except Track 2 / mixed at Dupa / Bergen / Norway
Mastered by Chris Blair at Abbey Road / London
Additional musicians:
Kjell Specter / Stig Pluto / David Aasheim / Gullet
Artwork: Martin Kvamme
Management: James Sandom at SuperVision

℗ & © 2002 Ultimate Dilemma
Distribution by 3MV/Pinnacle
+44 (0) 20 7378 8666
Made in England
www.ultimate-dilemma.com

magnet
CHASING
DREAMS EP

WHERE HAPPINESS LIVES /01
I'LL COME ALONG /02
HEAVIEST HEART /03
NOTHING HURTS NOW /04

UDRCDS048
www.HomeOfMagnet.com

All tracks written by Magnet
Copyright control
Tracks 1 & 4 Produced by Magnet
Tracks 2 & 3 Produced by Magnet and Sir Dupermann
Recorded and mixed at Magnetophonic Labs / Bergen / Norway
Except Track 2 / mixed at Dupa / Bergen / Norway
Mastered by Chris Blair at Abbey Road / London
Additional musicians:
Kjell Specter / Stig Pluto / David Aasheim / Gullet
Artwork: Martin Kvamme
Management: James Sandom at SuperVision

℗ & © 2002 Ultimate Dilemma
Distribution by 3MV/Pinnacle
+44 (0) 20 7378 8666
Made in England
www.ultimate-dilemma.com

magnet
CHASING
DREAMS EP

Enjoy
Tweeterfriendly
Music
Vol.2

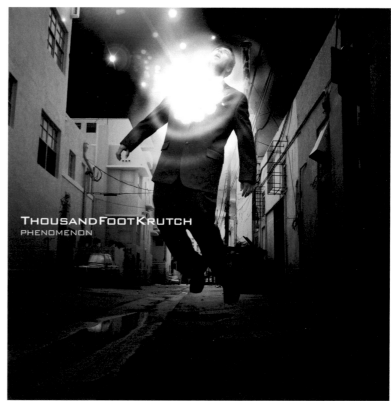

THOUSANDFOOTKRUTCH
PHENOMENON

velvet jones colin

Design	Play	Asterik	Stylorouge	Tsuyoshi Kusano
Music	Enjoy	Thousand Foot Krutch	Velvet Jones	Hanabi
Format	CD Cover	CD Cover	CD Cover	CD Cover

CATATONIA
INTERNATIONAL VELVET

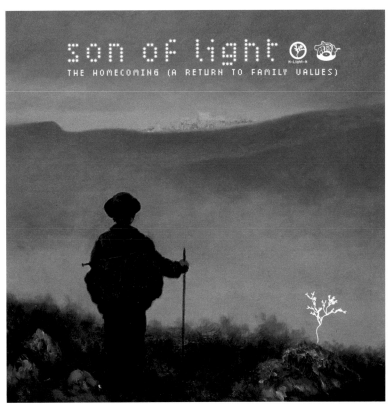

son of light   N-Light-N
THE HOMECOMING (A RETURN TO FAMILY VALUES)

Heather
Small.
PROUD

ECHO
& THE BUNNYMEN
WHAT ARE YOU
GOING TO DO
WITH YOUR LIFE?

Design   Stylorouge   Play
Music   Catatonia, Heather Small, Echo & the Bunnymen   Son of Light
Format   CD Covers   CD Cover   57

kingfisher/glass greece birds brick/winter. piano magic: mort aux vaches

limited, nr. 60? of 1000

ALL SONGS WRITTEN AND RECORDED BY PETER BOQOLUB AT HOME IN NEW YORK CITY DURING THE MONTHS OF 8/01-6/02. EXCEPT WHAT WAS SAID WHICH WAS RECORDED AND MIXED BY JEFF ZEIGLER IN PHILADELPHIA

GERARD ANGELINI PLAYED DRUMS ON WHAT WAS SAID AND MADELYN BURGESS SANG ON SPEAK SOFTLY. THIS ALBUM WAS MIXED BY MIKE TUCCHO AND MASTERED BY JIM DESALVO AT BEANSTUDIO MASTERING.

THE CD DIGIPACK WAS DESIGNED BY MULTIFRESH. ALL MUSIC IS COPYRIGHT THE SEMS / WWW.SEMSMUSIC.COM BUT THIS RELEASE IS COPYRIGHT AUDRAGLINT (AG107)

AUDRAGLINT
PORTLAND OREGON USA
WWW.AUDRAGLINT.COM

THE SEMS

THE SEMS
DRIFT
HARMLESS
STALKER BUT NICE
CURLEW
SPEAK SOFTLY
SUNNY DRIVE
BRIGHTER
IN THE MORNING LIGHT
RED SHIFT
WHAT WAS SAID
PLASTIC BOATS
SURE
SLUMBER

AG107

Design   A.Lorenz   mFresh
Music   Mort Aux Vaches Series The Sems
Format   CD Cover   CD Cover

58

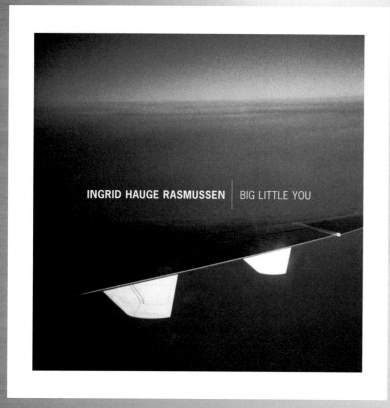

Design   Rune Mortensen
Music   Ingrid Hauge Rasmussen
Format   CD Covers

GUNNAR EIDE CONCERTS AS PROUDLY PRESENTS

LØRDAG 19 OKTOBER BETONG

DØRENE ÅPNER 20:00
FORSALG: BILLETTSERVICE/POSTEN: 815 33 133

betong

Design   Martin Kvamme
Music   Sigur Ros
Format   Gig Poster

MO
NOSU
RROUND
A01 GREEPY GUYS
A02 GREEPY GUYS
REMIX BY RACC
OON BROTHERS

versus

RA
CCOON
BROTHERS
B01 FINGERLICKING
GOOD B02 FINGER LI
CKING GOOD *REMIX*
BY MONOSURROUND

MONOSURROUND
versus RACCOON BROTHERS

Design   Maik Bluhm / 18.Oktober
Music   Various
Format   Vinyl Sleeves

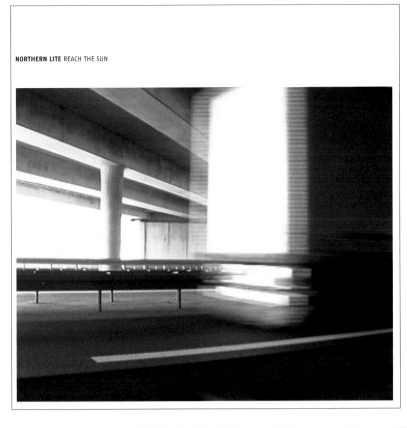

Gunjah Funkwelt EP

a1 Funkwelt a2 EF-Kondensat b1 430 Ost b2 Weniger Ist Weniger

Gunjah Funkwelt EP

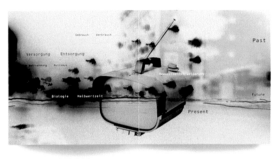

Design   Faktor
Music   Connected - Various
Format   CD Package

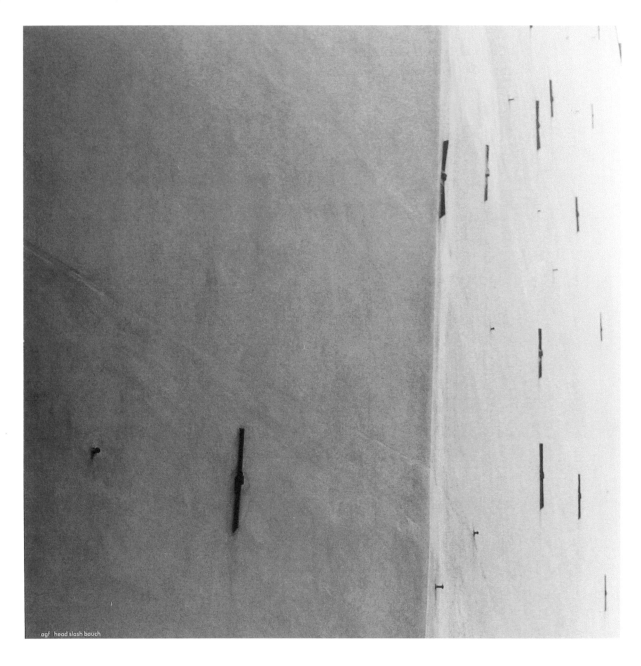

Design   A.Lorenz   mFresh
Music   agf   Fontanelle
Format   Vinyl Sleeve CD Cover

Design   A.Lorenz   Hydrafuse
Music   Electric Company   Robert Nanna/Elisabeth Elmore
Format   Vinyl Sleeve   Vinyl Sleeve

SVENSON
SEE YOU IN EARTH

Design   Io
Music   Svenson
Format   CD Cover

NITRADA 0+

Jullander
INTERIORS
Leute sehen hinaus. Innen ist
alles an seinem Platz.

01. THEME 1
NITRADA.COM/0+/0/

02. JUST CLOSE YOUR EYES
NITRADA.COM/0+/1/

03. THEME 2
NITRADA.COM/0+/0/

04. LE CHIEN QUI MANGE LA RUE
NITRADA.COM/0+/2/

05. THEME 3
NITRADA.COM/0+/0/

06. SKY WAS BLUE
NITRADA.COM/0+/3/

07. THEME 4
NITRADA.COM/0+/0/

08. LOVE ME
NITRADA.COM/0+/4/

NITRADA @ 2-ND.COM BERLIN HAMBURG WWW.2-ND.COM INFO@2-ND.COM

Design   Nitrada
Music   Nitrada, Jullander
Format   CD Covers

Slut

Nothing Will Go Wrong • Falling Down • I Can Wait
Time Is Not A Remedy • Easy To Love • Reminder
Universal • Something To Die For • Blow Up
One More Day • No Flowers, Please

Design   Factor Product
Music   Slut
Format   CD Cover, Book

Design	Factor Product
Music	Millenia Nova
Format	CD Cover, Book

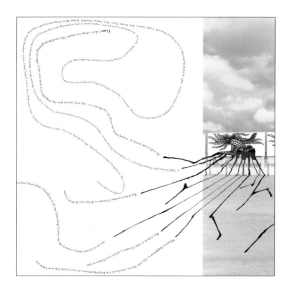

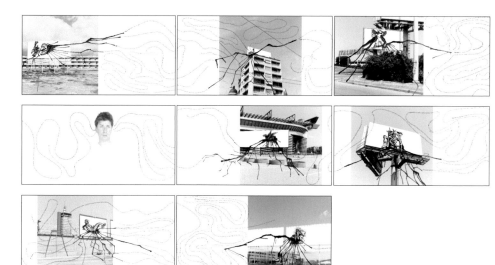

Design   Factor Product
Music   Thom
Format   CD Cover, Book

Design   Dirk Rudolph   Factor Product
Music   Reamonn   Emil Bulls
Format   CD Cover   CD Covers, Book

MAXIMILIAN HECKER
ROSE

MAXIMILIAN HECKER
DAYLIGHT

Design	A.Lorenz, Alexander Obst
Music	Maximilian Hecker
Format	CD Covers

NIO.
DO YOU
THINK YOU'RE
SPECIAL?

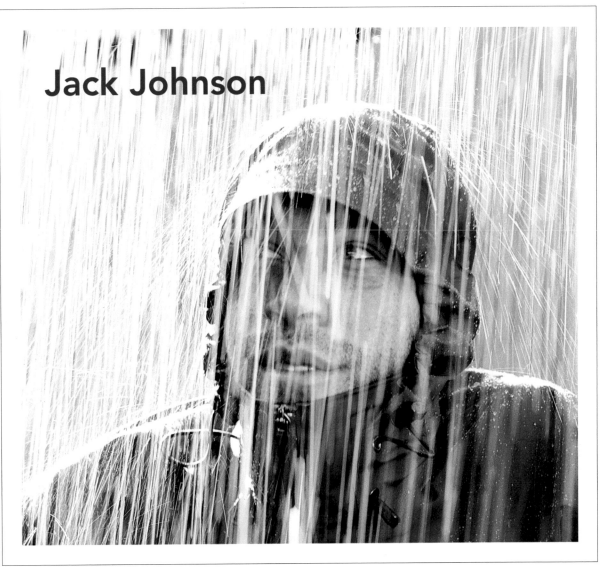

Jack Johnson

Batofar Tokyo 2001

Total Information: HEADZ (03-3770-5721)   http://www.faderbyheadz.com

Design	Big Active	Mike King	Surface	Akira Sasaki
Music	Nio	Jack Johnson	Auch	Batofar
Format	CD Cover	CD Cover	CD Covers	Flyer

75

him remix series #1:japan

Design	Kim Hiorthøy	Asterik	Fat Cat	Eh?
Music	Kim Hiorthøy	Norma	Him	DJ Signify
Format	CD Cover	CD Cover	Vinyl Sleeve	Vinyl Inner Sleeve

MIKE LINDUP . CONVERSATIONS WITH SILENCE

Design	Source	A.Lorenz	Stylorouge	mFresh
Music	Adrien	Donnacha Costello	Mike Lindup	Charles Atlas
Format	CD Cover	CD Cover	CD Cover	CD Cover

NORTHERN LITE
TREAT ME BETTER EP

01 TREAT ME BETTER *ORIGINAL VERSION*
02 MY PAIN *ALBUM VERSION*
03 EVERYBODY LOVES YOU *EP VERSION*
04 AWAY FROM YOU *ALBUM VERSION*
05 TREAT ME BETTER *EP VERSION*
06 TREAT ME BETTER *ENHANCED VIDEO*

LIMITED EDITION
5000 COPIES

WWW.NORTHERNLITE.DE
WWW.EASTWEST.DE
WWW.1STDECADE.DE

FRONT
ERIK NIEDLING
A_09, DIASEC, 166 × 130, 2000
WWW.ROTHAMEL.DE

5050466 854520

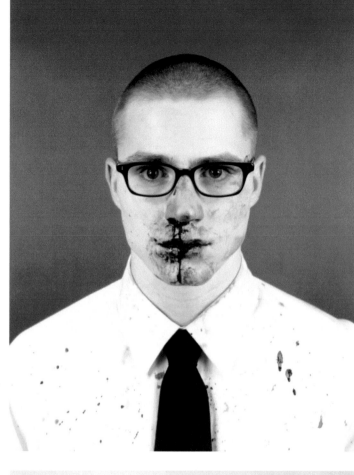

NORTHERN LITE TREAT ME BETTER EP

LC 01450 · 5050466.8545.2.0

NORTHERN LITE
TREAT ME BETTER EP

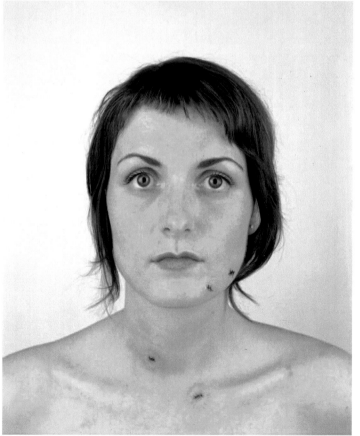

NORTHERN LITE MY PAIN

Design	Maik Bluhm / 18. Oktober
Music	Northern Lite
Format	CD Covers

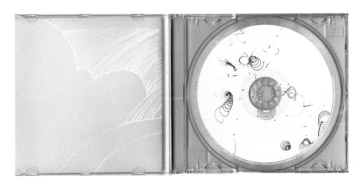

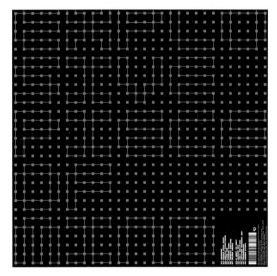

Design	Universal Everything	NonFormat	K7!	Pfadfinderei
Music	Tujiko Noriko	Cursor	Shantel	Ellen Alien
Format	CD Cover	Vinyl Sleeve	Vinyl Sleeve	Vinyl Sleeve

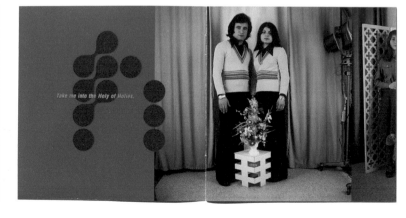

Design	Zion	Fons Hickmann
Music	Eclectic Bob	Nonex
Format	CD Cover	CD Cover

Design   KarlssonWilker
Music   Eftir Bögn
Format   CD Cover, Book

EINSTÜRZENDE NEUBAUTEN PERPETUUM MOBILE

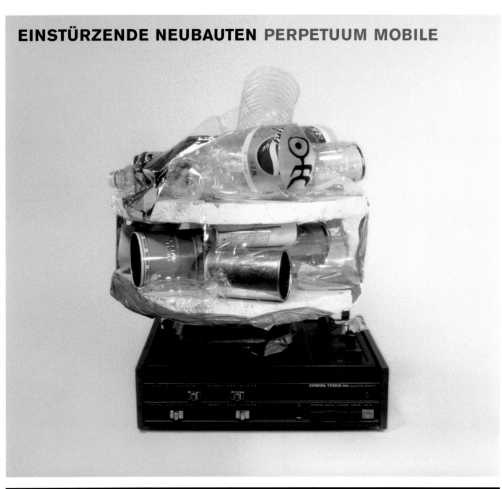

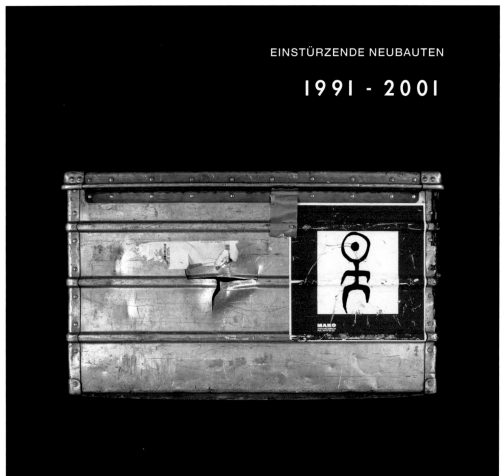

Design   Minus
Music   Einstürzende Neubauten
Format   CD Covers

9-15-2000, BRUSSELS

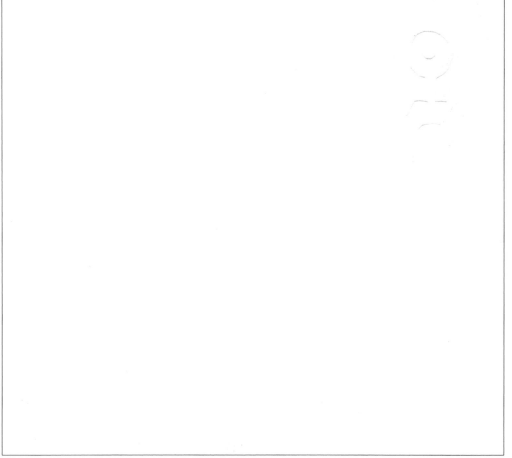

Design	Zion	Stylorouge	Factor Product
Music	User	The Ordinary Boys	Tomcraft
Format	CD Cover	CD Cover	CD Cover

Jim O'Rourke
I'm happy and I'm singing and a 1,2,3,4

Jim O'Rourke: I'M HAPPY, AND I'M SINGING, AND A 1,2,3,4

COVER BY FRANK: ANIMALS FOR KING

Mego 050

Mego 050

© MEGO 2001 > > > WWW.MEGO.AT

SOME KIND OF KINK.
RED SNAPPER°

Design	Tina Frank	Apt. 13	Red	Rune Mortensen
Music	Jim O'Rourke	The Hal of Shedad	Red Snapper	Muo
Format	CD Cover	CD Cover	CD Cover	CD Cover

85

Design	Rune Mortensen
Music	Jazz CD Compilation
Format	CD Package

JR EWING
RIDE PARANOIA

JR EWING
RIDE PARANOIA

01 REPETITION IS FAILURE
02 WHEN YOU'RE GONE
03 MIDNIGHT EPISODE
04 NAKED PAVEMENTS
05 PRE SUMMERTIME BLUES
06 A CASE OF EVACUATION
07 LAUGHING WITH DAGGERS
08 SWEET
09 ELECTRIC YESTERDAY
10 THE EXACT SAME THING
11 4:00 AM
12 AN INTRODUCTION TO ...
13 ... RIDE PARANOIA

JR EWING
RIDE PARANOIA

Design   Rune Mortensen
Music   J.R.Ewing
Format   CD Cover, Book

Design   Robert Samsonowitz
Music   Plej
Format   CD Cover, Book

88

Design Spezialmaterial
Music   Spezialmaterial Compilation
Format CD Cover

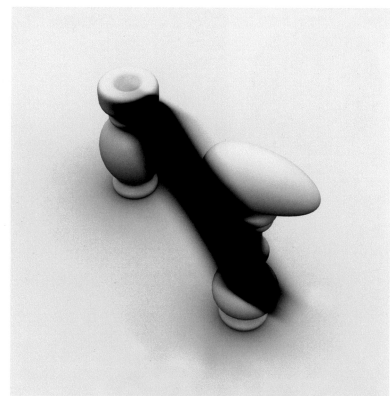

Design Hideki Inaba
Music   e2-e4
Format Vinyl Sleeve

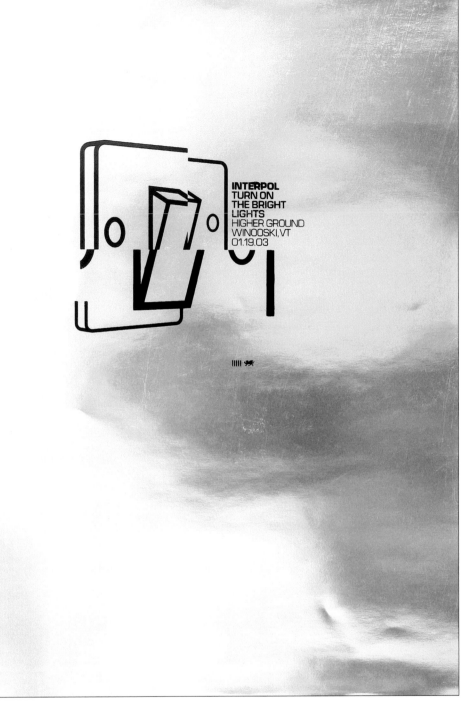

**INTERPOL
TURN ON
THE BRIGHT
LIGHTS
HIGHER GROUND
WINOOSKI, VT
01.19.03**

opensource.code

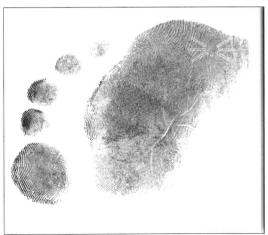

Design	Superlow	JDK	Source	Icon
Music	Earth 2	Interpol	Open Source	Jürgen De Blonde
Format	Vinyl Sleeve	Gig poster	CD Cover	CD Cover

SONO2000GUNS

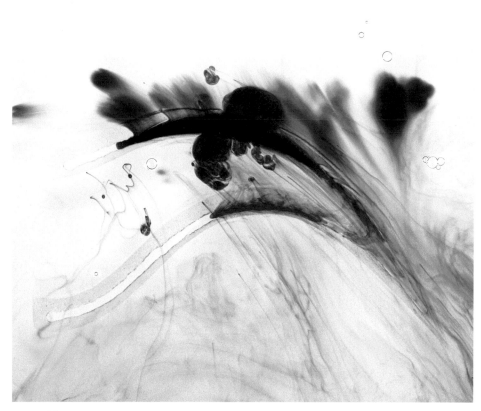

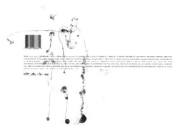

Design   Dirk Rudolph
Music   Sono
Format   CD Covers, Books

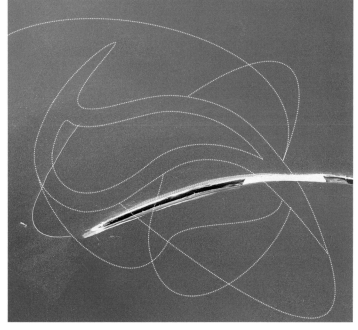

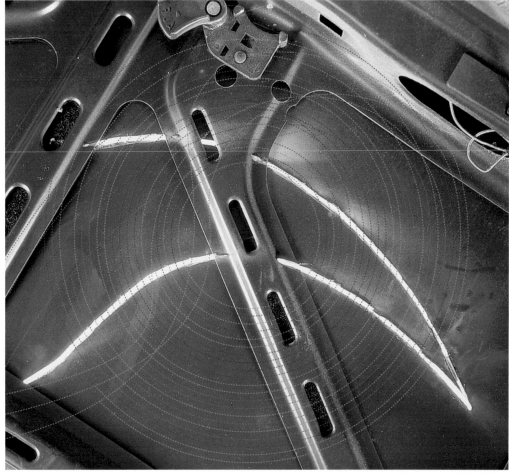

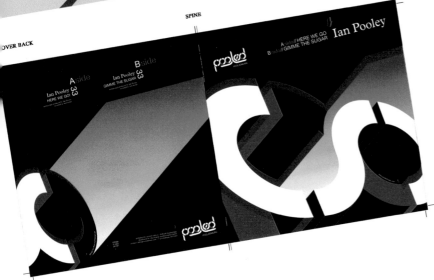

Design	Wuff Design	Pfadfinderei	Burnfield
Music	Labelcover Pooledmusic	Sascha Funke	Drink
Format	Vinyl Sleeves	Vinyl Sleeves	Poster

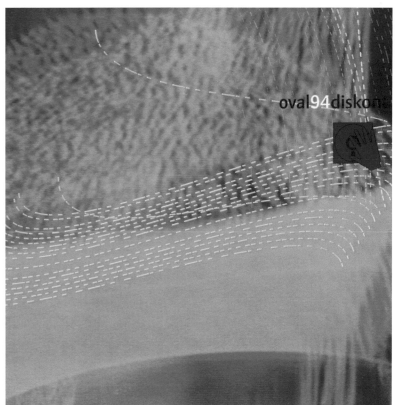

Design	Sue Garner	Oval	Hydrafuse
Music	Sue Garner	Oval	Mates of State
Format	CD Cover	CD Cover	CD Cover, Poster

SPAN
FOUND

PAPA
SPAN

SPAN

DON'T THINK THE WAY THEY DO

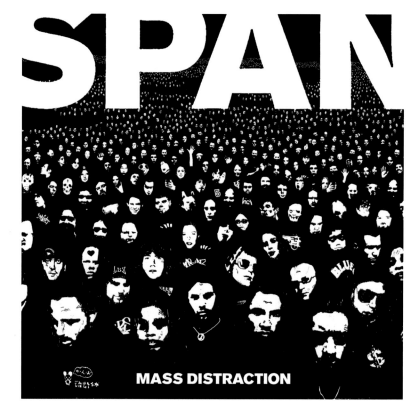

SPAN

MASS DISTRACTION

SPAN

MASS DISTRACTION

Design   Big Active
Music   Span
Format   CD Covers

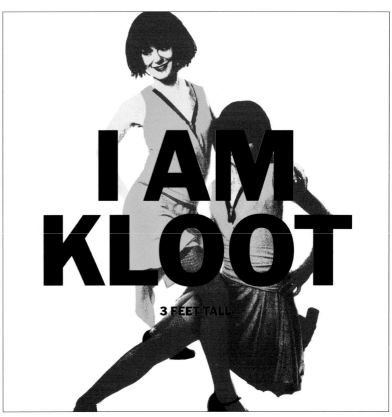

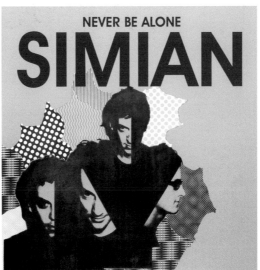

Design   Big Active
Music   I am Kloot, Simian
Format   CD Covers

97

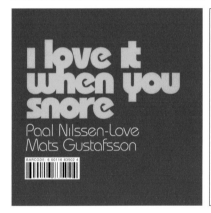

Design	moss design unit	Büro Destruct		NonFormat	Struggle	Dirk Rudolph	Rune Mortensen	Io	So Takahashi	
Music	Cosmic Village	V. Scientists, Give Peas, L. Vibert, Ninjatune		Luke Vibert	Mos Def	Lambretta	Paal Nilssen-Love	Caesars Palace	Nubus	
Format	CD Cover, Vinyl Sleeve	Flyer		Vinyl Sleeve	Vinyl Sleeve	CD Cover	CD Cover	CD Cover	CD Cover	98

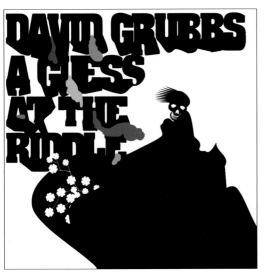
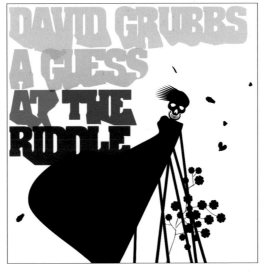
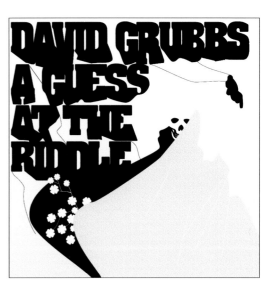

Design   Kim Hiorthøy
Music   Jaga Jazzist, David Grubbs
Format   CD Covers, Vinyl Sleeves

Tigerbeat6

Design   Slang International
Music   Kid 606, Gold Chains
Format   Vinyl Sleeves

Design   National Forest
Music   Lé Sound in Color Series
Format   CD Covers

101

TENTEKI2002 / (–::::T:T::::–)

SOLOTEMPO (LIVE / SCHWEIZ / SPEZIALMATERIAL)
WWW.SPEZIALMATERIAL.CH
ROB HALL (SPECIAL-GUEST-DJ / ENGLAND / GESCOM_SKAM)
WWW.SKAM.CO.UK
SM-DJ'S (DJ'S / SCHWEIZ / SPEZIALMATERIAL)
WWW.SPEZIALMATERIAL.CH
26-04-2002 / 22.00 UHR
BOA KULTURZENTRUM LUZERN / BOA BAR

TENTEKI2002 / (–::::T:T::::–)

SOLOTEMPO (LIVE / SCHWEIZ / SPEZIALMATERIAL)
WWW.SPEZIALMATERIAL.CH
INTRICATE (LIVE / SCHWEIZ / SPEZIALMATERIAL)
WWW.SPEZIALMATERIAL.CH
ROB HALL (SPECIAL-GUEST-DJ / ENGLAND / GESCOM_SKAM)
WWW.SKAM.CO.UK
SM-DJ'S (DJ'S / SCHWEIZ / SPEZIALMATERIAL)
WWW.SPEZIALMATERIAL.CH
JEE (DJ / DEUTSCHLAND / AB.ART-SOUNDSYSTEM)
WWW.AB.ART.DE
27-04-2002 / 22.00 UHR
PATHOS TRANSPORTTHEATER MÜNCHEN / DACHAUERSTRASSE 110 D / 80636 MÜNCHEN

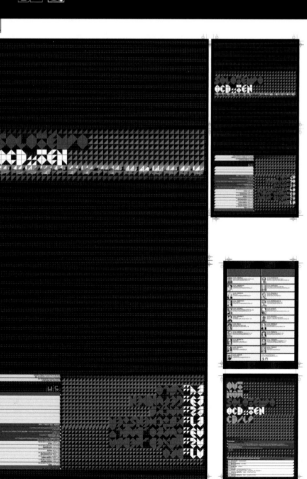

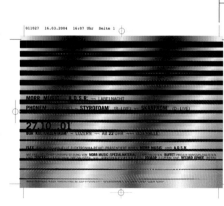

Design   Spezialmaterial
Music   Various
Format   Flyers

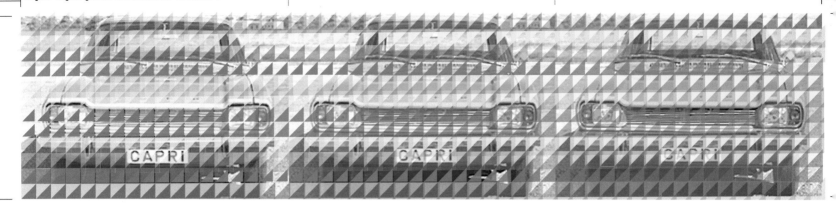

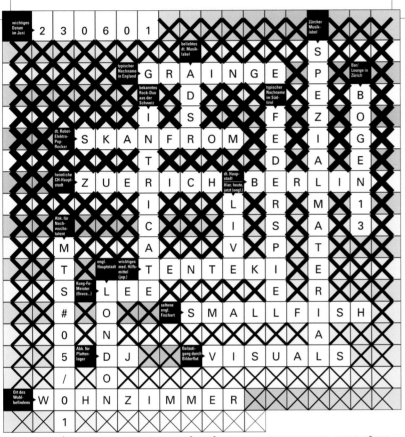

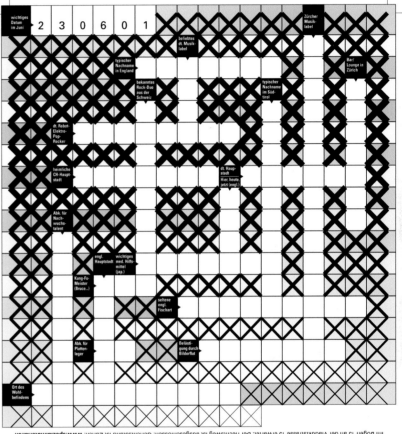

Design	Spezialmaterial	Akira Sasaki
Music	Various	Scanner + D-Fude
Format	Flyers	Flyer

103

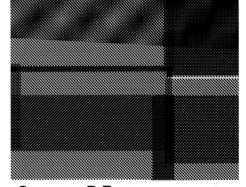

Scanner + D-Fuse
JAPAN TOUR : 2/9 (Fri) at Shinjuku MARZ (03-3202-8248) | OPEN / START 23:30- | advance ¥2800, door ¥3300

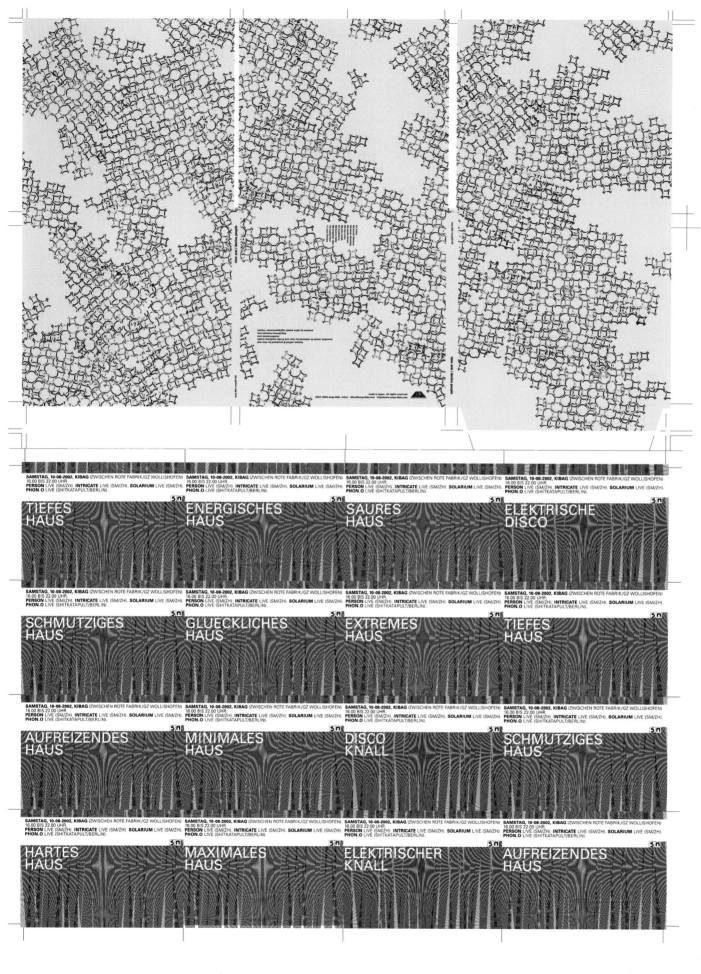

Design   Akira Sasaki   Spezialmaterial
Music   Riow Arai   Various
Format   CD Cover   Flyers

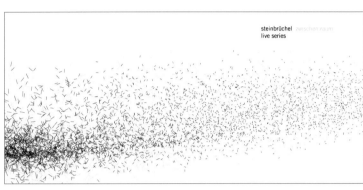

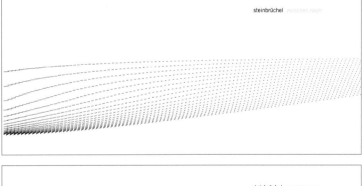

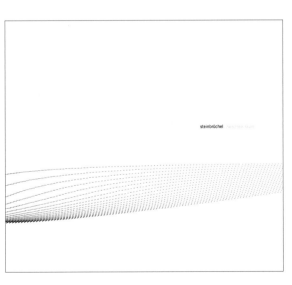

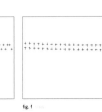
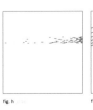

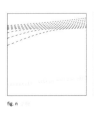

fig. b   fig. d   fig. f   fig. h   fig. j   fig. l   fig. n   fig. p   fig. r

Design   John Wiese   Knat FM   Nicolas Bourquin
Music   John Wiese   Apparat   Steinbrüchel
Format   Vinyl Sleeve   Vinyl Sleeve   CD Cover, Bock, Label, Poster

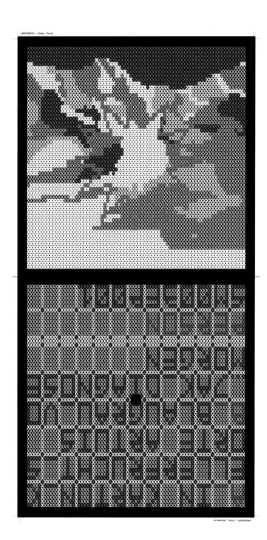

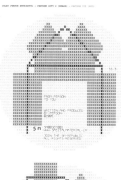

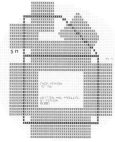

IT'S UNBEARABLE!

SPEZIALMATERIAL PRÄSENTIERT: UNBEARABLE RECORDINGS
FREITAG, 16.11.2001 – HEINRICHSTRASSE 137, AB 22.30 UHR
LIVE: **GAMERS IN EXILE** (IT; UNBEARABLE), **GOODIEPAL** (DK; UNBEARABLE/V-VM TEST), **SOLARIUM**
AKA **HOOVERCRAFT3000** (CH; SPEZIALMATERIAL/7B). DJ'S: **TORDIS BERSTRAND** (IT; UNBEARABLE),
ASA (D; INSINE.NET/FONTFORES.DE) UND **SPEZIALMATERIAL-DJ'S**. DON'T MISS, IT'S UNBEARABLE!

EINLASS MIT FLYER. UNKOSTENBEITRAG CHF 10.–

Design   Spezialmaterial
Music   Various
Format   Vinyl Sleeve, Flyer

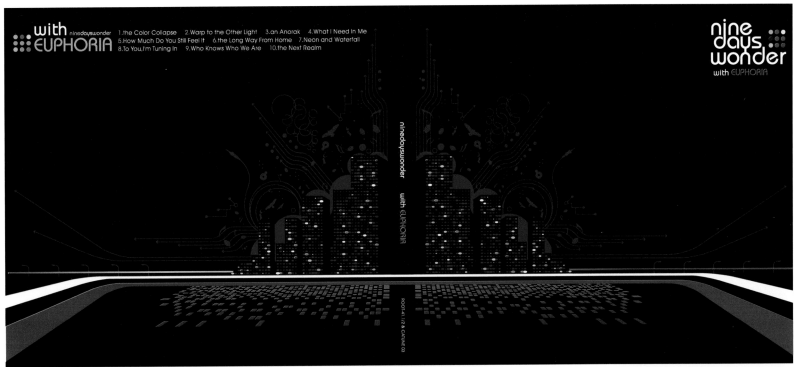

with **EUPHORIA** ninedayswonder 1.the Color Collapse 2.Warp to the Other Light 3.an Anorak 4.What I Need In Me 5.How Much Do You Still Feel It 6.the Long Way From Home 7.Neon and Waterfall 8.To You,I'm Tuning In 9.Who Knows Who We Are 10.the Next Realm

nine days wonder with EUPHORIA

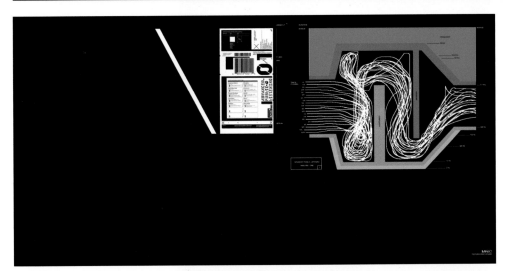

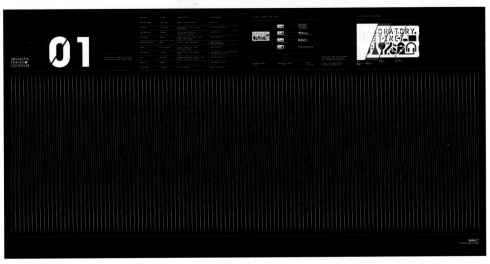

Design	Regina	Universal Everything	Ralph Steinbrüchel
Music	Nine Days Wonder	Lab 01	Steinbrüchel/Brusa
Format	Vinyl Sleeve	Vinyl Sleeve	Packaging

107

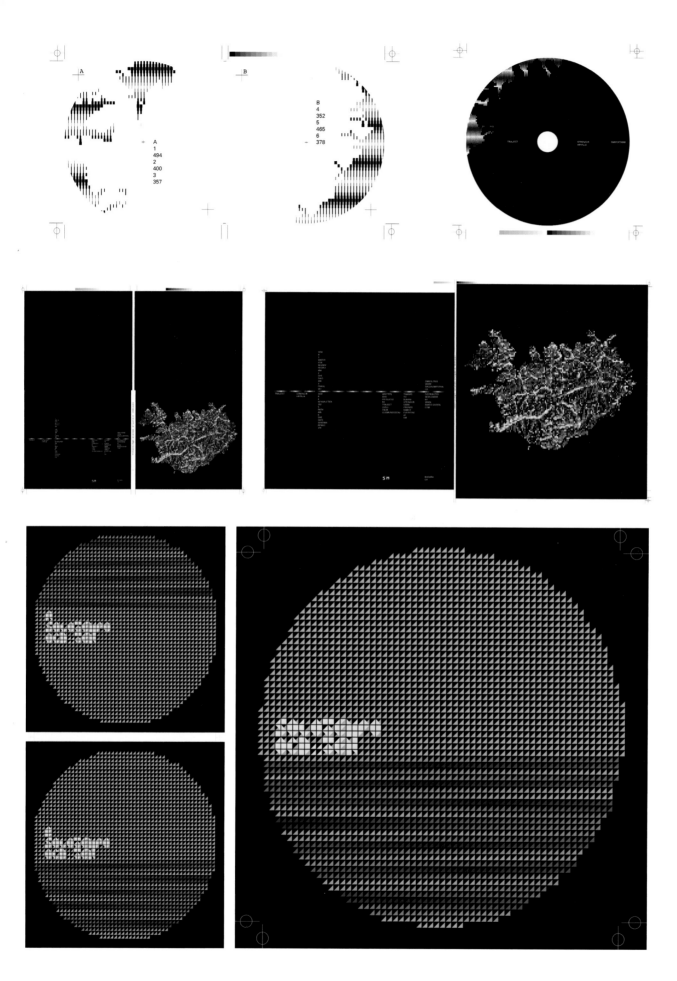

Design   Spezialmaterial
Music   Various
Format   Vinyl Sleeves

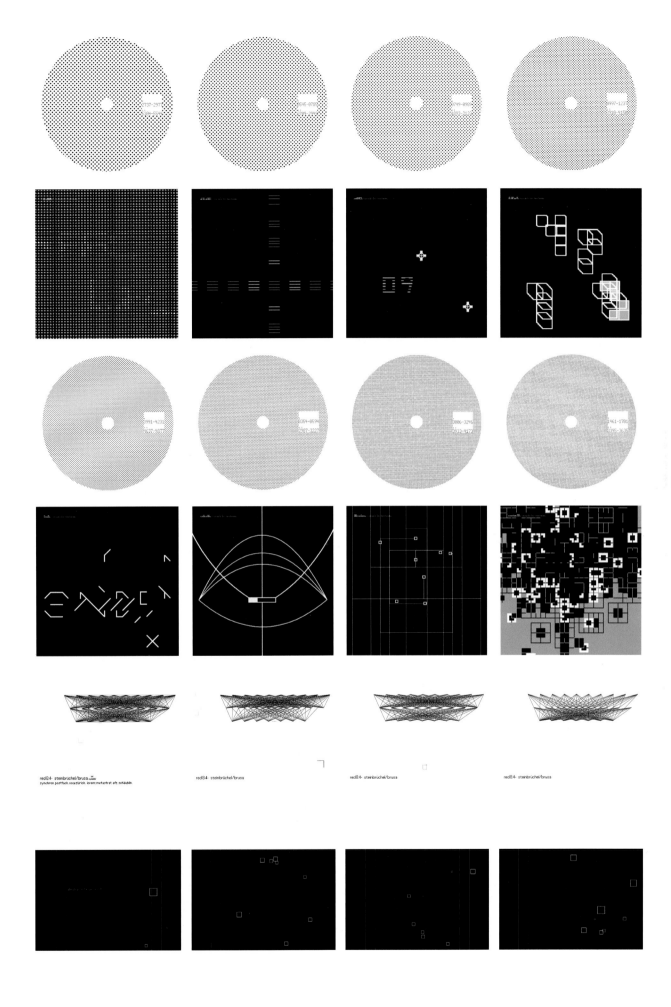

Design   Ralph Steinbrüchel
Music   Various
Format   Vinyl Sleeves

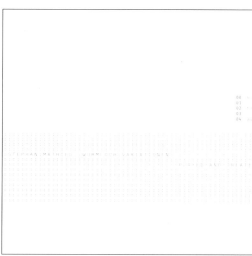

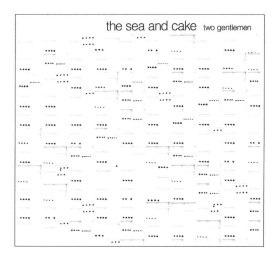

the sea and cake two gentlemen

Design   A. Lorenz   The Sea and Cake   mFresh
Music   Various   The Sea and Cake   Kid 606
Format   Vinyl Sleeves   CD Cover   Gig Poster

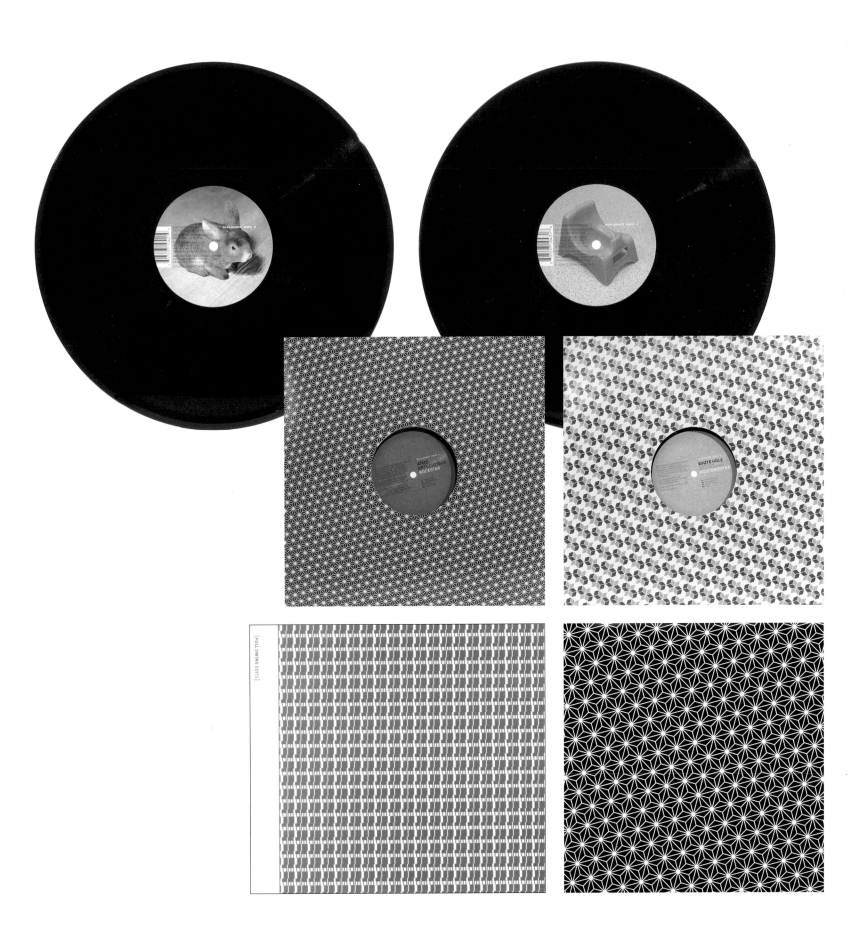

Design   A. Lorenz
Music   Various
Format   Vinyl Sleeves, CD Covers

C118715-02 ▶

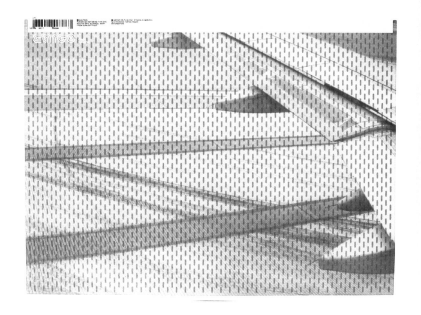

The Militia:
Weight Gain EP
1/2 Parts*

Cargo
Industries

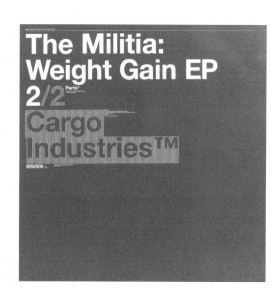

The Militia:
Weight Gain EP
2/2 Parts*

Cargo
Industries™

Design   D-Realm
Music   Various
Format   Vinyl Sleeves

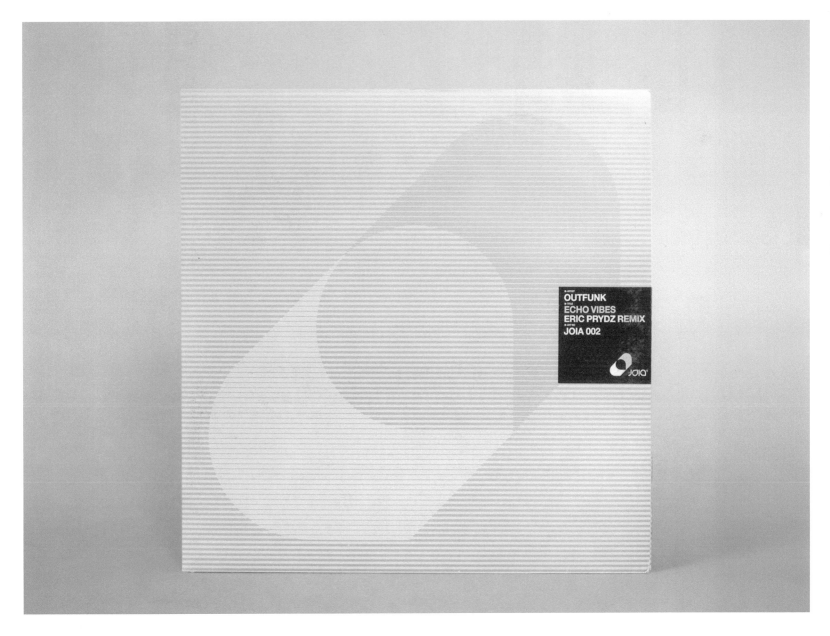

Design   Surface   Zion
Music   Cocoon Compilations Outfunk
Format   Vinyl Sleeves   Vinyl Sleeve

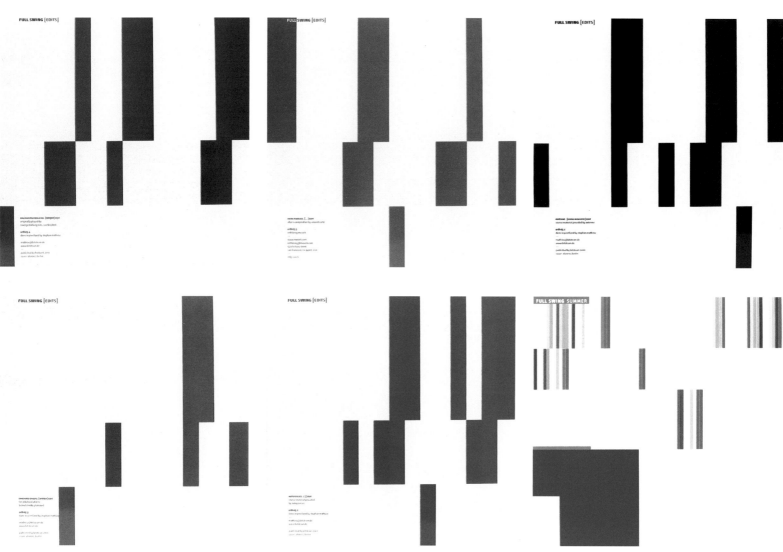

Design   A.Lorenz
Music   Various
Format   Vinyl Sleeves

114

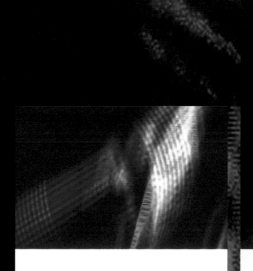

rechenzentrum *Director's Cut*

P and C Mille Plateaux 2003. www.mille-plateaux.com. LC 10521.
Weserstrasse 7 D60339 Frankfurt/Main, Germany. act@force-inc.com T 49(0)69 23 99 18 F 49(0)69 25 72 80 EFA 73170–2 MP 120

rechenzentrum

rechenzentrum *Director's Cut*

rechenzentrum

rechenzentrum *The John Peel Session*

rechenzentrum *The John Peel Session*

Design   A.Lorenz
Music   Rechenzentrum
Format   CD Covers, Vinyl Sleeves, Posters

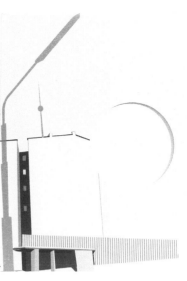

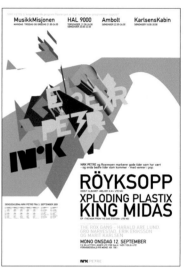

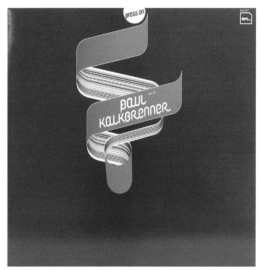

Design	Pfadfinderei	Rune Mortensen
Music	Various	Röyksopp
Format	Vinyl Sleeves	Poster

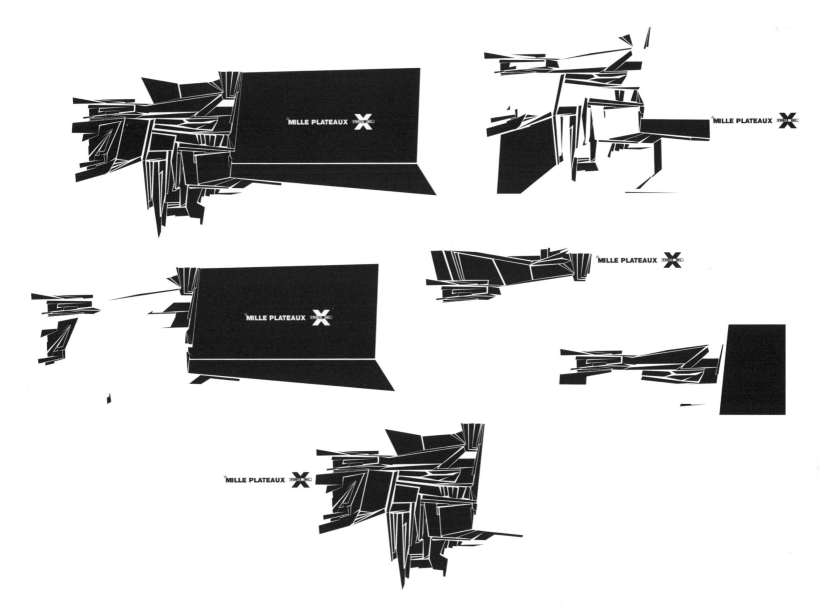

Design   Akira Sasaki
Music   Mille Plateaux/Force Inc. - Various
Format   Flyer, T-Shirt, Images

Design   Monitor Pop
Music   Various
Format   CD Covers

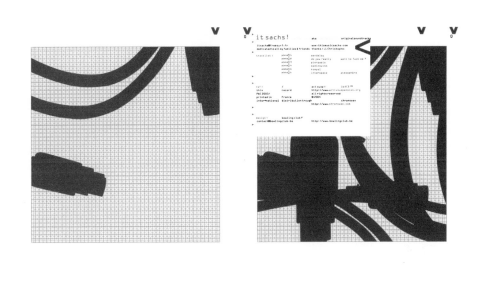
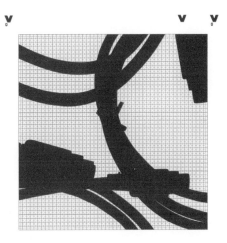

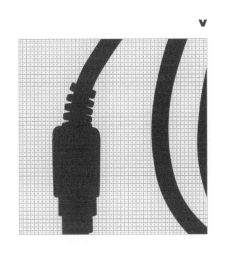
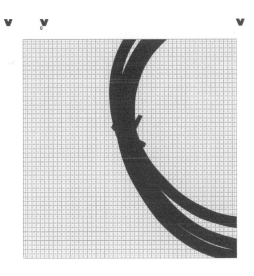
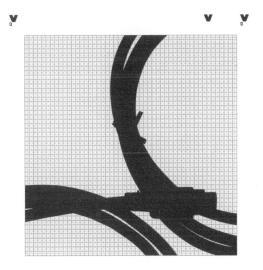

Design   Bowling Club
Music   It Sachs!
Format   CD Cover

THIS POSTER ANNOUNCES A NEW BAND WITH A NEW SOUND:

ECCENTRICITY–TOUR

THE BAND IS:

SANDIE WOLLASCH – VOCALS | NKETCHI MBAKWE – VOCALS

SEBASTIAN STUDNITZKY – TRUMPET | OLI RUBOW – DRUMS

HELLMUT HATTLER – BASS

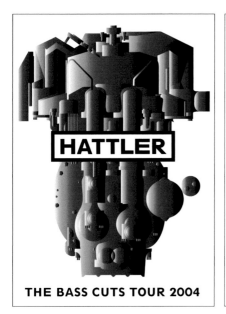

THE BASS CUTS TOUR 2004

THE BASS CUTS TOUR 2004

Design   KarlssonWilker
Music   Hattler, Elemental Chill Series
Format   CD Covers, Posters

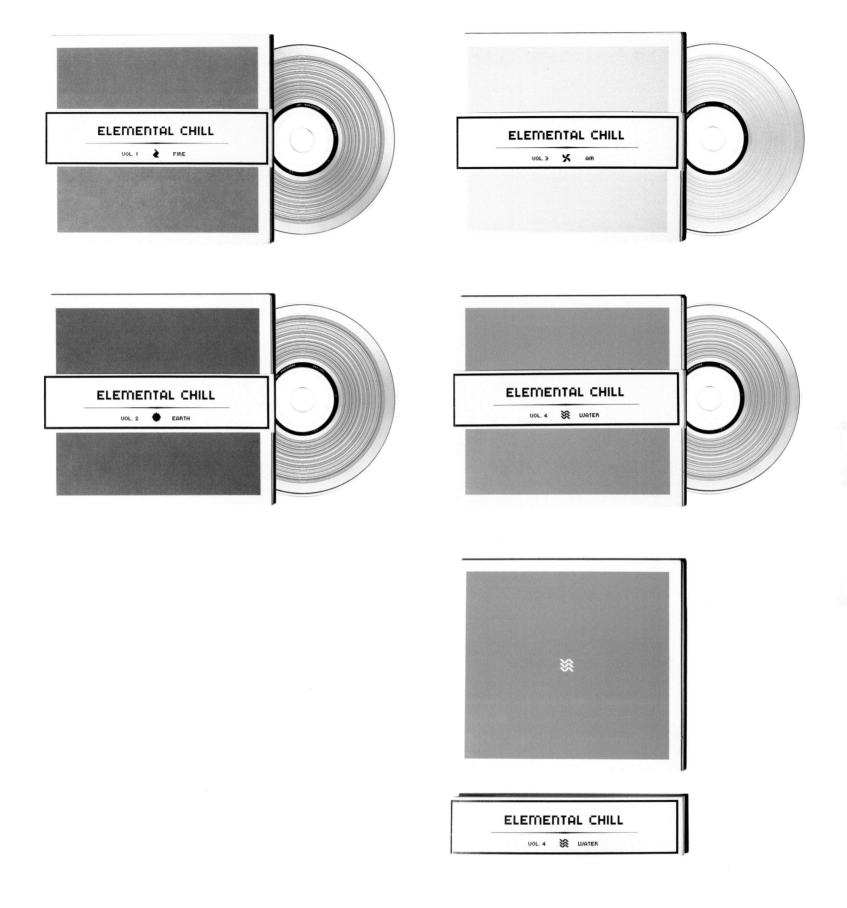

KRAAN LIVE 2001

MOTION UNIT_MY MIND

grafik.marcus

My Mind / Club Mix	7:13 min
My Mind / Dj I.C.O.N. Remix	6:07 min
In The Land Of Funk	6:49 min
My Mind / Radio Edit	3:26 min

All tracks written by André Winter & M. Hatzler
produced by André Winter & M. Hatzler
Published by Alstermusikverlag

licensed from Confused Recodings

This s a   Production

Design   KarlssonWilker   Disko Döner
Music   Kraan   Motion Unit
Format   CD Cover, Poster CD Cover

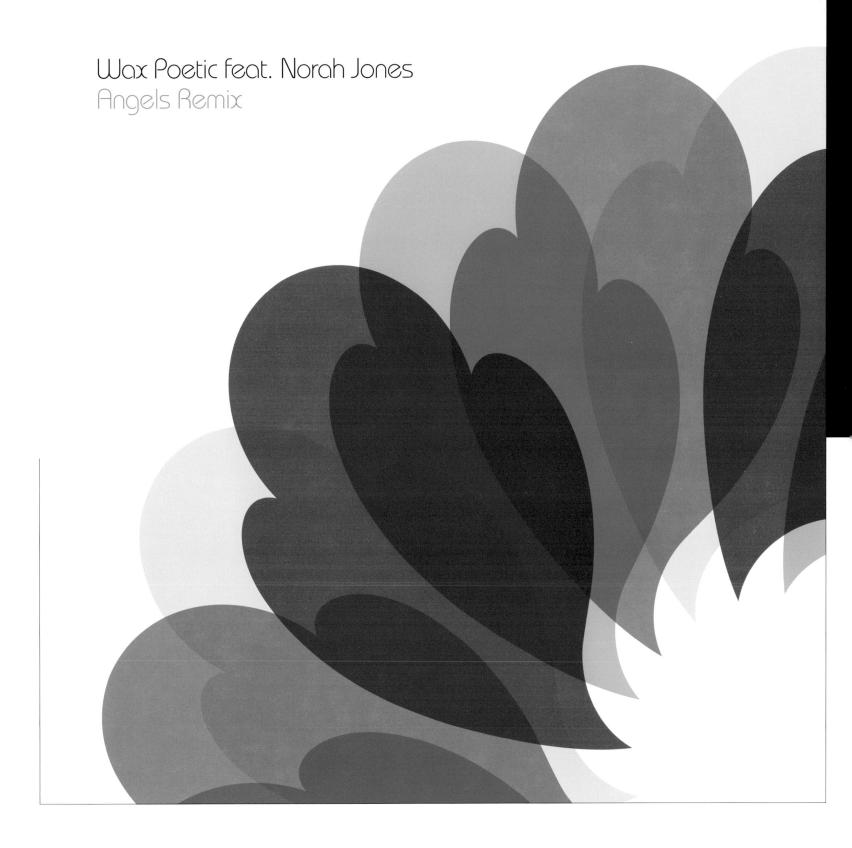

Wax Poetic feat. Norah Jones
Angels Remix

Design   Airside
Music   Wax Poetic
Format   Vinyl Sleeve

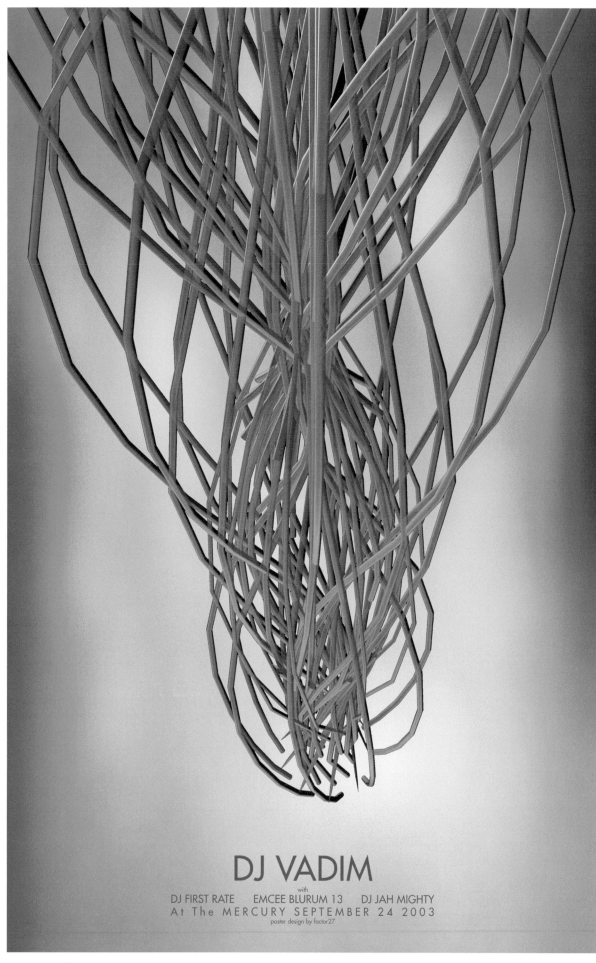

DJ VADIM

with

DJ FIRST RATE   EMCEE BLURUM 13   DJ JAH MIGHTY
At The MERCURY SEPTEMBER 24 2003
poster design by factor27

Design   F27
Music   DJ Vadim
Format   Gig Poster

OUTWARD MUSIC COMPANY {AND} CARPARK {PRESENT}
NUDGE {CD RELEASE}
TAKAGI MASAKATSU
GLOMM {AND} METATRON
THURSDAY NOVEMBER ONE
PORTLAND BLACKBIRD

Design   mFresh
Music   Nudge
Format   Gig Poster

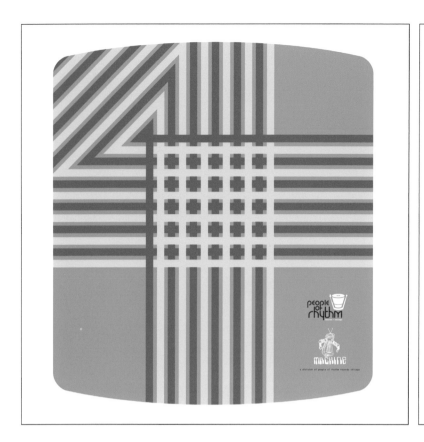

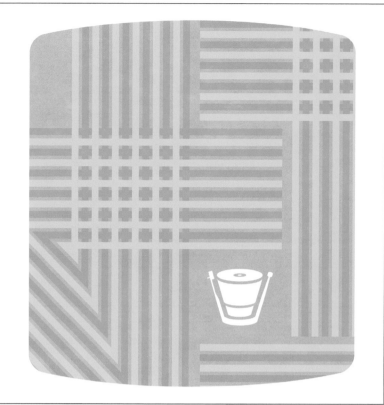

Design	Struggle	Red
Music	People of Rhythm	Terry Callier
Format	Vinyl Sleeve	CD Cover

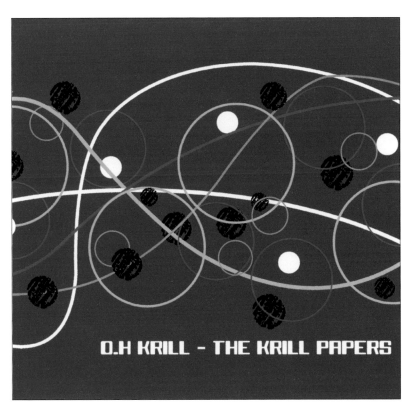

O.H KRILL - THE KRILL PAPERS

TOM TYLER   THE RIGHT INFORMATION

STEVE LACY   ROSWELL RUDD
monk's dream

with
jean-jacques avenel   john betsch   irene aebi

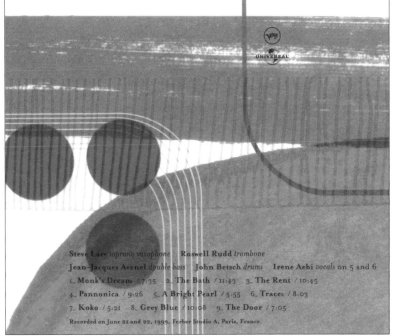

Steve Lacy *soprano saxophone*   Roswell Rudd *trombone*
Jean-Jacques Avenel *double bass*   John Betsch *drums*   Irene Aebi *vocals* on 5 and 6
1. Monk's Dream / 7:35   2. The Bath / 11:43   3. The Rent / 10:45
4. Pannonica / 9:26   5. A Bright Pearl / 5:55   6. Traces / 8.03
7. Koko / 5:21   8. Grey Blue / 10:08   9. The Door / 7:05
Recorded on June 21 and 22, 1999, Ferber Studio A, Paris, France.

Design   Dag
Music   Various
Format   CD Covers, Vinyl Sleeves

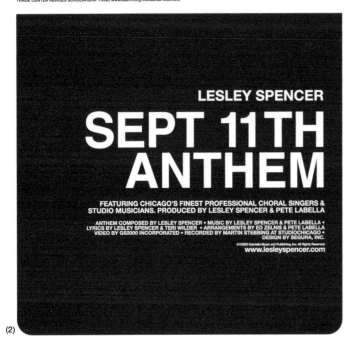

(3)

(2)

(1)

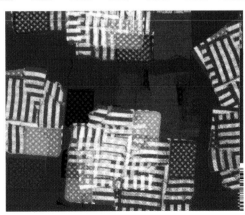

Design   Tortoise   Fat Cat
Music   Tortoise   Xinli Supreme
Format   CD Cover   CD Cover

THEY DON'T WANT TO UPSET THE APPLECART

THEY DON'T WANT TO CAUSE ANY HARM

BUT IF YOU DON' WAN'T LIKE WHAT THEY'RE GOING TO DO

YOU'D BETTER NOT STOP THEM 'COS THEY'RE COMING THROUGH

PAGE 1 / 2

PAGE 3 / 4

PAGE 5 / 6

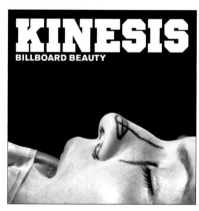

PAGE 7 / 8

PAGE 9 / 10

PAGE 11 / 12

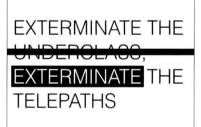

EXTERMINATE THE
~~UNDERCLASS,~~
EXTERMINATE THE
TELEPATHS

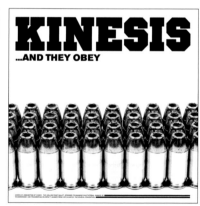

KINESIS
BILLBOARD BEAUTY

KINESIS
...AND THEY OBEY

Design	Tsuyoshi Kusano	Big Active
Music	Collider, Exterminate	Kinesis
Format	Various	CD Covers

130

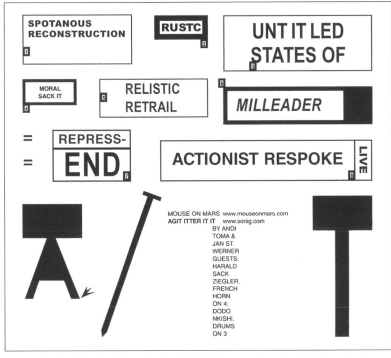

Design Icon
Music   Mouse on Mars, Sonig Compilation
Format CD Covers

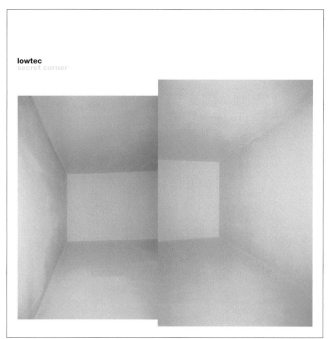

lowtec
secret corner

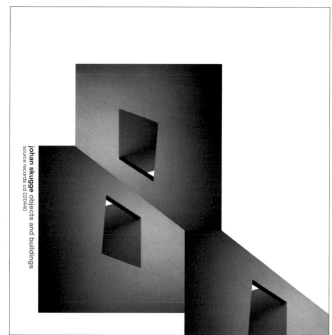

johan skugge objects and buildings
source records cd 02040

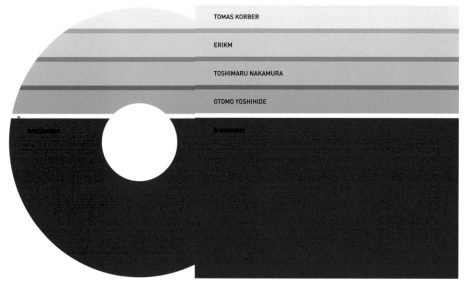

TOMAS KORBER

ERIKM

TOSHIMARU NAKAMURA

OTOMO YOSHIHIDE

brackwater

brackwater

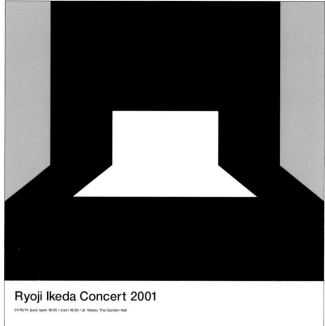

Ryoji Ikeda Concert 2001
01/10/14 (sun) open 18:00 / start 18:30 / at Yebisu The Garden Hall

Design	Env	Akira Sasaki	Ralph Steinbrüchel
Music	Lowtec, Johan Skugge	Ryoji Ikeda	Various
Format	CD Covers	Flyer	CD Cover

kid606 ps you love me

kid606 ps I love you

MONOPOT   TARAN E.P.   STS048CD

Design	A.Lorenz	Rune Mortensen
Music	Kid 606	Monopot
Format	Vinyl Sleeves	Vinyl Sleeve

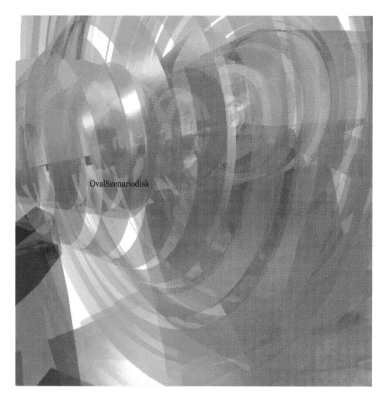

SAY NO TO PRIMATE   RESEARCH LABS

OvalSzenariodisk

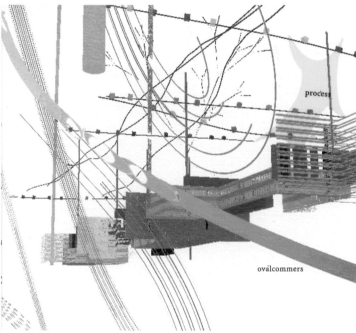

process

ovalcommers

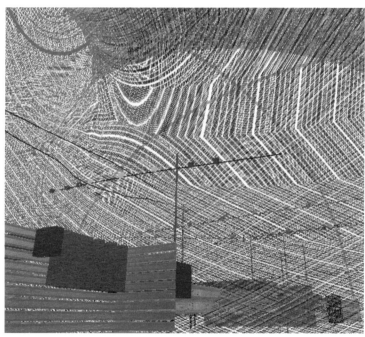

mouse on mars

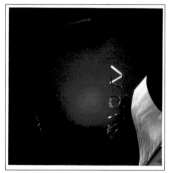

Design	Icon	Boogizm
Music	Various	Fym
Format	CD Covers	CD Cover

134

Flim, Helio

ART OF FIGHTING WIRES

Giardini di Mirò

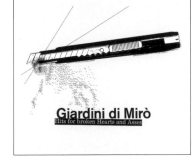

Design	Universal Everything	Normal	Silke König	David Schellnegger	Hydrafuse
Music	Flim	Art of Fighting	Giardini di Miro	Giardini di Miro	Aloha
Format	CD Cover	CD Cover	CD Cover	CD Cover	CD Cover

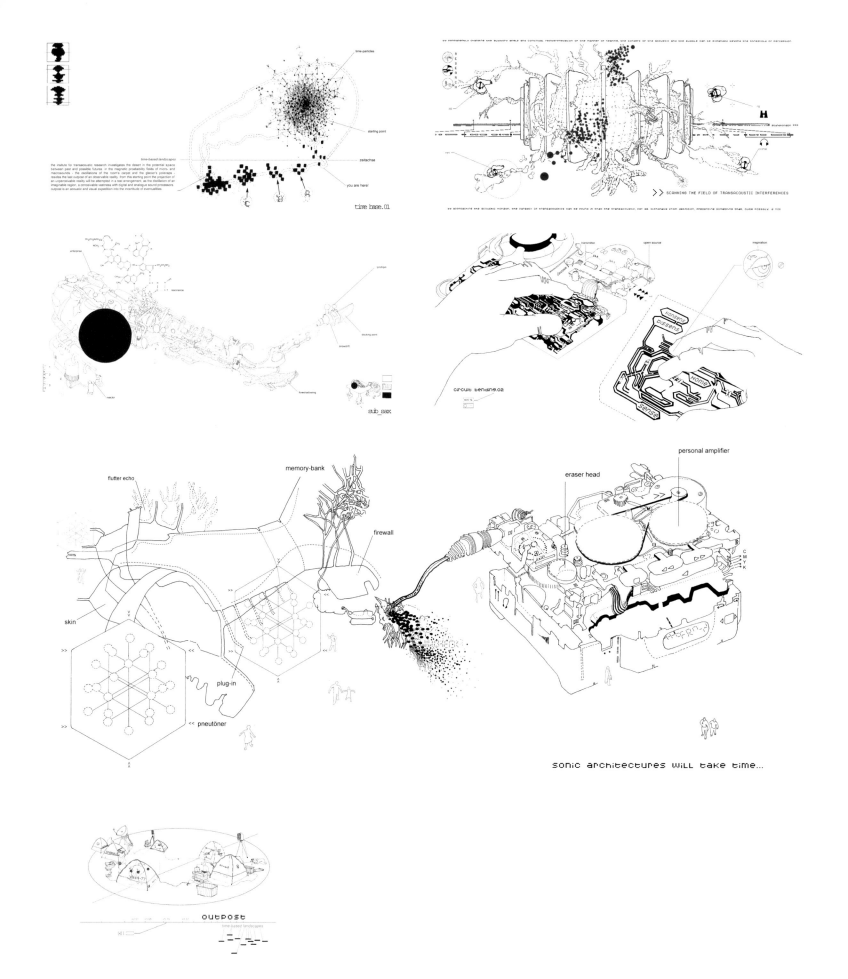

Design   Transacoustic Research
Music   Outpost
Format   CD Cover

PREFUSE-73
intro
Produced by Prefuse 73

MOS DEF & DIVERSE
wylin out (kutmasta kurt mix)

AESOP ROCK
train buffer (aesop rock mix)

ATMOSPHERE
fear

DIVERSE
blindman (low budget mix)

CAURAL
photograph

PREFUSE-73
interlude
Produced by Prefuse 73

THE TIMEOUT DRAWER
broad grins from the boarding ramp

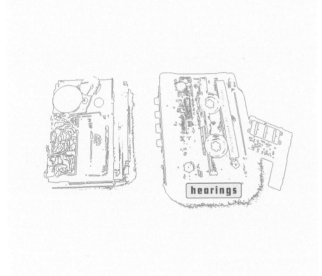

Design	Struggle	Transacoustic Research	Burnfield
Music	Urban Renewal Programm	Hearings	Role Model
Format	CD Cover	CD Cover	CD Cover

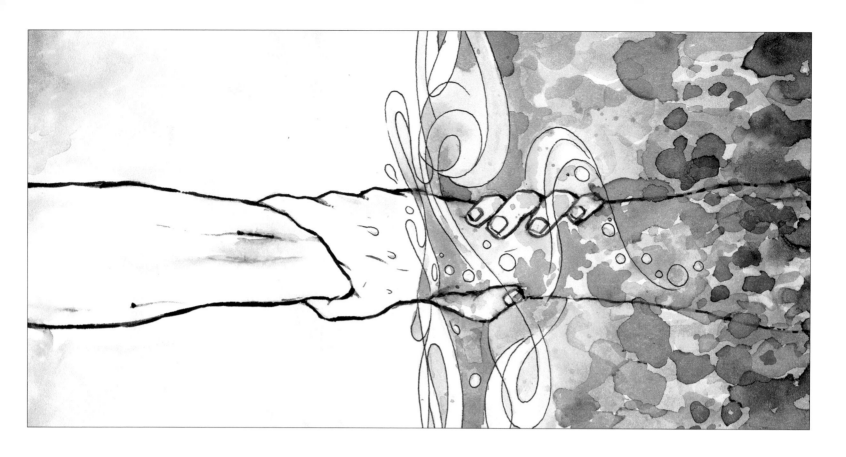

stacs of stamina
pilot balloon
isn't this enough
hug dusty / throe stasis
vampire tonic

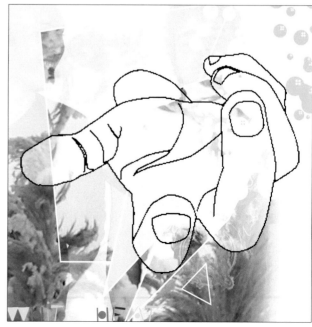

Design	Dan Abbott	Johan and Jethro	Infoplop
Music	Mars Volta	Stacx of Stamina	White Heat
Format	CD Book Illustration	Vinyl Sleeve	CD Cover

ナーヴ・カッツェ Nav Katze
Never mind the distortions

Remixed by Aphex Twin, Autechre, Black Dog, Sun Electric, Ultramarine,
Global Communication, Reload, μ-Ziq, Seefeel, Disjecta, The Gentle People

Great Remix Album of Electronic
2CD
2003.09.03 ON SALE

VICP-62424-25 ¥3,150 (TAX IN) Victor Entertainment, Inc. http://www.jvcmusic.co.jp

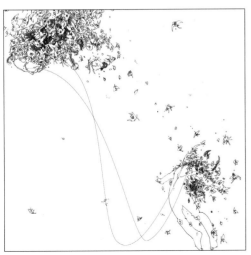

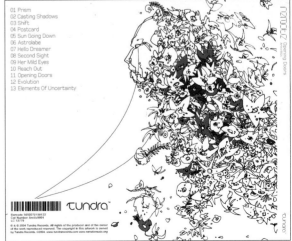

01 Prism
02 Casting Shadows
03 Shift
04 Postcard
05 Sun Going Down
06 Astrolabe
07 Hello Dreamer
08 Second Sight
09 Her Mild Eyes
10 Reach Out
11 Opening Doors
12 Evolution
13 Elements Of Uncertainty

Design	Hideki Inaba	Zip
Music	Nav Katze	Remote
Format	Flyer	CD Cover

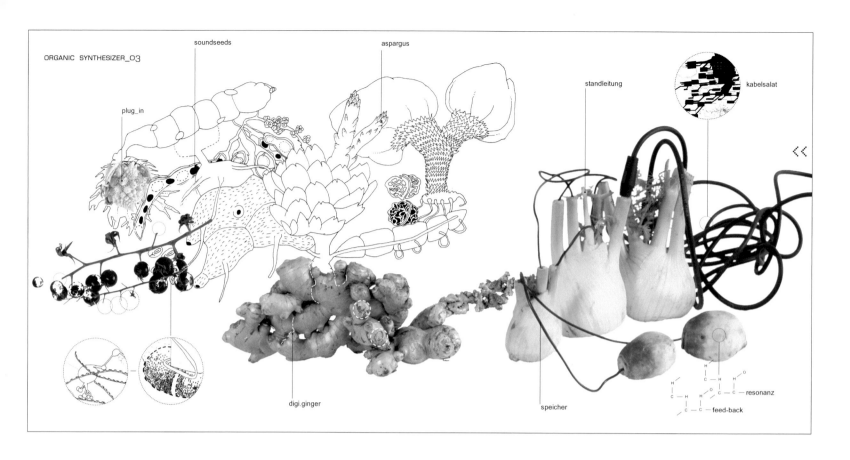

ORGANIC SYNTHESIZER_03

plug_in

soundseeds

aspargus

standleitung

kabelsalat

digi.ginger

speicher

resonanz

feed-back

SILICON SOUL

pouti

MOTIVATION EATING SWEETS

Design	Transacoustic Research	Disko B	Enlightenment
Music	Organic Syntesizer	Pouti	Motivation
Format	CD Book	CD Cover	CD Cover

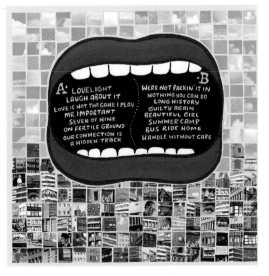

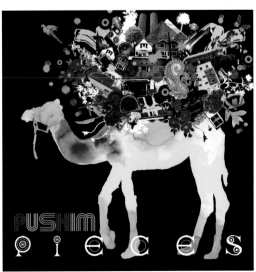

Design	Ingoranz	Dan Abbott	Tomoko Tsuneda
Music	Die Türen	Mind Kiosk	Pushim
Format	CD Cover	CD Cover	CD Cover

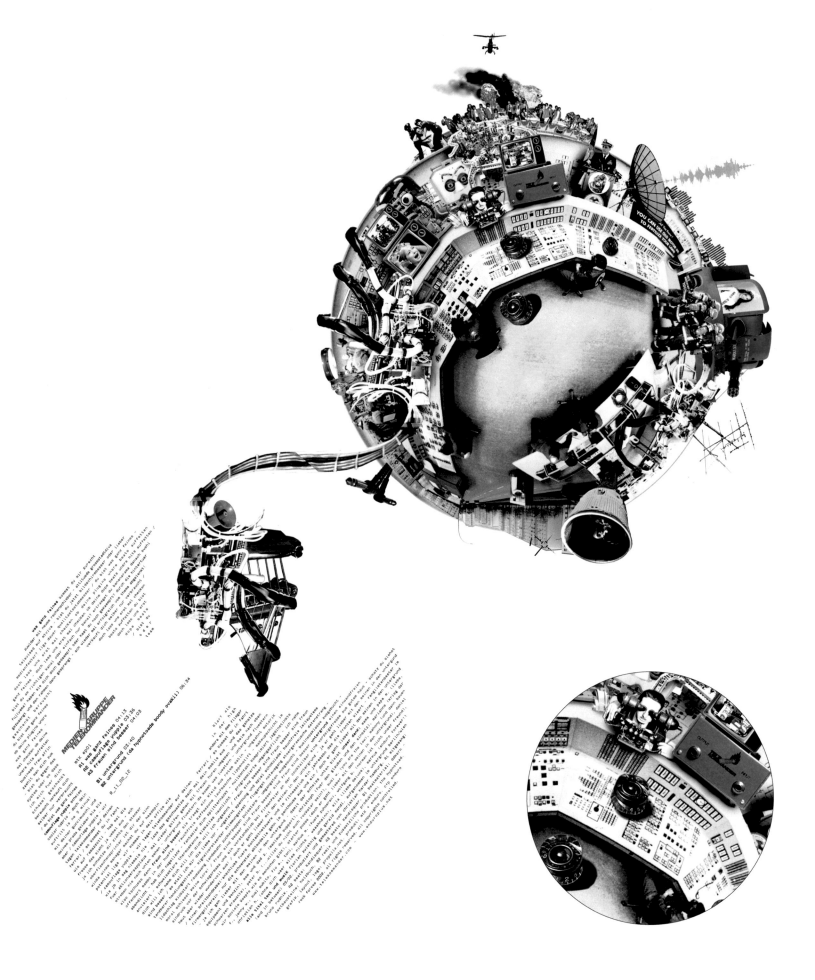

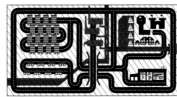
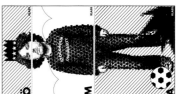

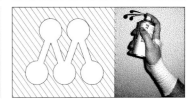

Design   Sweden
Music   Dr. Kosmos
Format   CD Cover, Book, Poster

Ultraschall   Feb. 2002

Ultraschall   April 2002

Ultraschall   April 2002

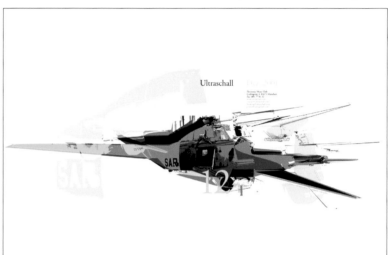

Ultraschall

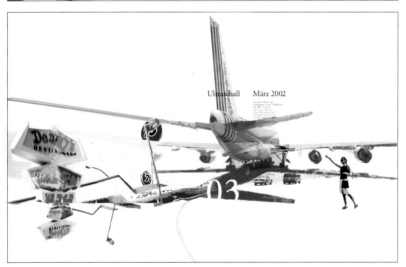

Ultraschall   März 2002

Ultraschall   Juni 2002

Design   Faktor
Music   Überschall
Format   Flyer

CREDO

Rafael Toral / Alejandra & Aeron
2003.7.18 (fri) at SUPER DELUXE

open 18:00/start 19:00 advance ¥3000, door ¥3500 (1 drink order)

Rafael Toral, Alejandra & Aeron, Aki Onda, minamo

Total Information: HEADZ (03-3770-5721)

6 Jahre
Ultraschall²
Samstag 14.09.2002

ULTRASCHALL

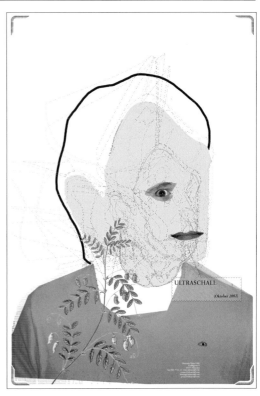

Design	Faktor	Akira Sasaki	Tsuyoshi Hirooka	
Music	Various	Rafael Toral, Alejandra & Aeron	Kitchen	
Format	Flyer, Poster	Flyer	Flyer (street cone artwork)	145

Design   Shrine
Music   Fuel
Format   Illustrations

146

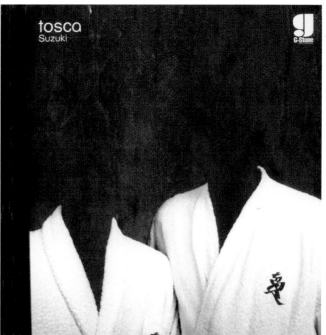

Design	Big Active	Sarah Littasy
Music	Pleasure	Tosca
Format	CD Covers	CD Cover

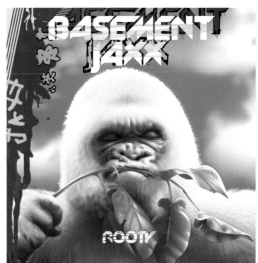

Design   Big Active
Music   Basement Jaxx
Format   CD Covers

BLUEJEANS

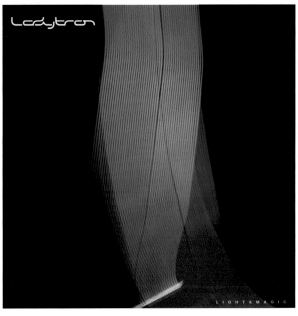

Design   Big Active
Music   Ladytron
Format   CD Covers

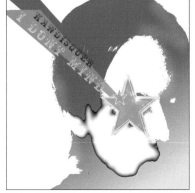

Design   Ingoranz   Tsuyoshi Hirooka
Music   Various   Too Darn Cool, Teenage of the Year
Format   CD Covers   CD Covers

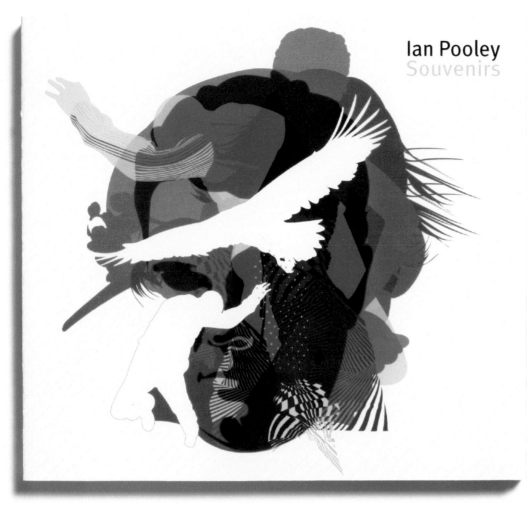

Ian Pooley
Souvenirs

自らの作品を他者の感性に委ねてみる。それはまた自らを省みることに他ならない。
"Future In Light" に対する、彼ら気鋭アーティストの映像的、音像的な解釈（Interpretation）を集めたのがこの作品集だ。（ケンイシイ）

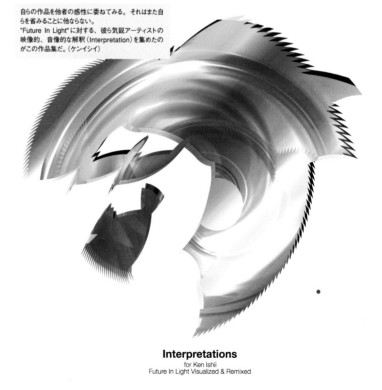

Interpretations
for Ken Ishii
Future In Light Visualized & Remixed

Design	Wuff	Tsuyoshi Kusano
Music	Ian Pooley	Ken Ishii
Format	CD Cover, Book	CD Cover

10
2003
7
11
23:00—

BECK
SEA CHANGE TOUR
2002-2003

Design	Tsuyoshi Hirooka	Laurent Fetis	Karen Ingram
Music	Teenage of the Year	Beck	Tussle
Format	Flyers	Tour Poster	CD Cover

Design   Rocking Jelly Bean
Music   Thee Michelle Gun Elephant
Format   Tour Poster

Design   Honest
Music   Ween
Format   Web Illustration

155

Design	Fat Cat	Transacoustic Research
Music	Sigur Ros	Rough Mixes
Format	CD Cover	CD Cover

Design   Fat Cat   Pfadfinderei
Music   Sigur Ros   Alex Amonn
Format   CD Cover   Vinyl Sleeve

157

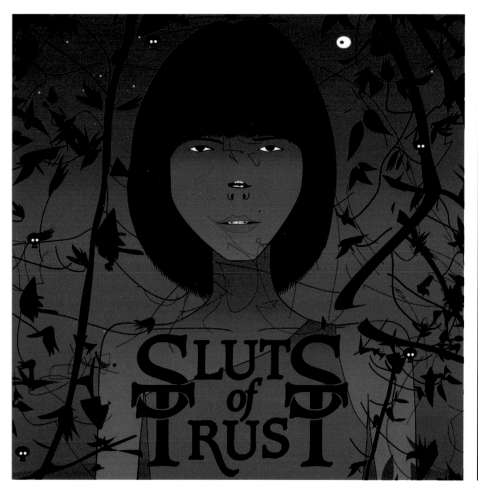

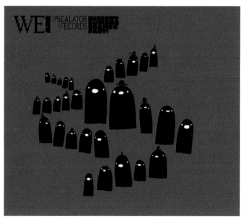

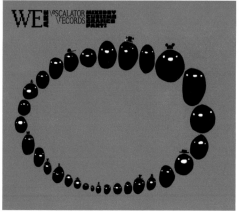

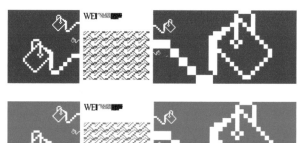

Design	Thomas Barwick	Tomoko Tsuneda	Syrup
Music	Sluts of Trust	Dixied The Emons	Escalator Compilation
Format	CD Cover	Vinyl Sleeve	CD Cover

Design   Seb Jarnot
Music   Llorca
Format   CD Cover, Poster

Design   Büro Destruct
Music   Various
Format   CD Cover

KULTURHALLEN
DAMPFZENTRALE

BEJAZZ

WINTERFESTIVAL 22.-25. JANUAR 2004

DO 22.01. WORLD NIGHT
FR 23.01. FUTURE NIGHT
SA 24.01. SATURDAY NIGHT
SO 25.01. FINAL NIGHT

WWW.BEJAZZ.CH

VORVERKAUF: TICKETCORNER

ILLUSTRATION UND GESTALTUNG
MERIDIANER-BÜRO DESPERGT MERAK CAPITAL

Design   JDK
Music   Ween, Tenacious D.
Format   Gig Poster

COSMOS
TAKE ME WITH YOU

Design   Zip
Music   Cosmos
Format   Promo

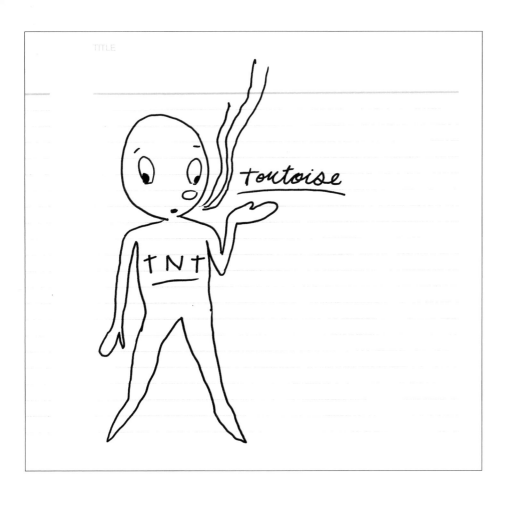

Design	Tortoise	Fons Hickmann
Music	Tortoise	Hauschka
Format	CD Cover	CD Cover

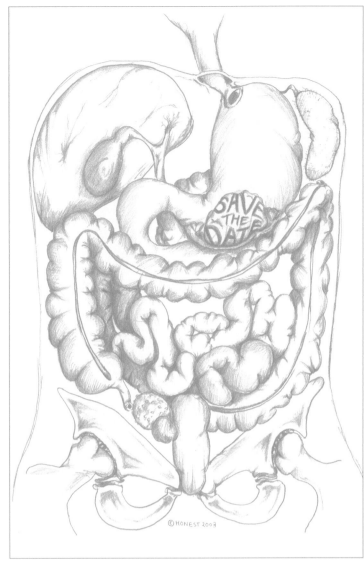

Design	T. Stout	Big Active	Honest
Music	Trouble Everyday	Violent Delight	Saves the Day
Format	Poster	CD Covers	Illustration

Design	Dennis Tyfus	T. Stout	MRZ
Music	Trumans Water, Cassini Division	Unwound, The Ex	Massimo
Format	Single Sleeve, MC Sleeve, Single Sleeve	Tour Poster	CD Cover

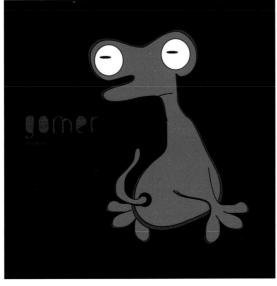

Design	Insect	Rinzen	Pury
Music	Monk & Canatella	Bananageddon, Singles	Gomer
Format	CD Cover	Poster, CD Cover	Vinyl Sleeve

169

Once upon a time in the west...

...in Ytre Arna, Bergen, Norway around 1975 a young redneck was born. His biggest interests were cowboys and Indians, western movies, and music. The movies might not have been that great but the young boy had a vision and the future in front of him.

BACK IN NORWAY in those days there was only one choice for television entertainment... God Bless NRK. They used to show movies on Mondays and something called 'Detectlve' hour on Friday nights. There wasn't even a slight chance for Ho Hibbed to get her youngster to bed before the show was over. Fiedent she must have been...

A FEW YEARS later this young boy adopted the name Brighton Gay.
This was his idea of a cool Cowboy-Chief name for hanging out and playing with his best mates. It's quite intriguing as this young man couldn't speak a word of English and had not been introduced to school yet.
One day his love for the western life got overshadowed by the growing interest for playing instruments and becoming a famous rockstar.

BRIGHTON STARTED HIS first band "clean roads" together with Boris Flashback and his bigger bro at the age of 9. He undoubtedly believed the band would have WORLD DOMINATION within the next few years of his life... but it didn't work out that way. After this BG played with several bands, some named and others unnamed. All successful according to himself. He floated through life with the motto 'Sometimes things happen for a reason, things you never expected or planned'. This leads us to CoStar.

SO THE BIG question is who and what is CoStar! CoStar is a group of people that put together for a reason. When the purpose is done they might not see each other for awhile. It's still the same intensity as if it was your normal band situation. The outlaws might change, and the music with it. This is why CoStar has it's own life.

IN THE FUTURE anything can happen, but one thing is certain: the BROTHERS IN CRIME EP is out in Jan 2003. So look out for CoStar!

Brighton Gay
Brighton Gay, Jan 2003

As I touch you I find I'm scared to.

I wake up as the sun alights me, I close my eyes to rest but I cant sleep. By my side you're still sleeping, I'm trying not to make a sound, easier said than done. And now I'm willing to steal your precious sleep, and as I touch you I find I'm scared to. Allow me hands to touch again, dead quiet as I am I still breath. By my side no luck could change your talking in your sleep, as the sun moves all over you. And now

I'm willing to steal your precious sleep, and as I touch you I find I'm scared to. And I am full aware of the silence, more of my own beauty. More of your beauty. More of your beauty. More of your beauty. And now I'm willing to steal your precious sleep, and as I touch you I find I'm scared to.

I'll give it all I've got, cause I got time and space for you.

As one of Brighton's named bands naturally folded and faded quietly he decided to move away from the usual band formula. He decided to use one of his early visions to put a gang of outlaws together and play music. This idea led to the creation of the CoStar 'Brothers in Crime' EP. It was an easy effort. He just got a few parts together, hanging around in the studio making sure that the feel was right. People came by. Some made it on to disc, others didn't. But an EP came out of it.

I'm sure I've told you, you can have everything. I'll give it all I've got, cause I got time and space for you. You are special and you should know. You are special and you should know. You got the power, you can change everything. You have talent, enough for all of us. But you cant see it, that's why I'm here for you. I'm here to tell you, you've been blind so long. If you give all you have to offer, the impossible will

be possible. If you give all you have to offer, the impossible will be possible. I'm sure that I've told you, you're special and you should know. So listen up my friend, you know you got the gift And if someone else will tell you, that I was wrong today, tell them that you're special, that's all you have to say. This is not a broken promise, and this is not a lie, that's all I have to tell you today.

Cause now I know, my love burns like a fire.

I should have known by now. By now. I should have known by now. That I should take a change cause I may lose it. If I can change your mind. If I can change your mind. Then I let it climb disappear so it's unreachable. I leave it with my fear. Cause now I know, my love burns like a fire. I'm able to believe... you will come around. This time, you will come around. This time, you will come around.

4 3 2 1 ZERO!

COUNT DOWN AND GET READY FOR COSTAR ISSUE NO.1

LOVE AND FIRE, HORNS AND ORDER, CLASS AND COMFORT MIXED INTO A TASTEFUL MUSICAL SALAD FOR YOUR ENJOYMENT

BROTHERS IN CRIME EP OUT NOW!

SUPPORT THE FIGHT AGAINST WRONG

I think this is the time of my life.

It's good to be around you this life. I love it here, Peaking, This is how I want it to be. Nothing compare to how I'm breathing, I'm alive and it's real. I mean lightly, Peaking, I think I understand what it means. A nice way to change everything. A nice way to change everything. A nice way to change everything... cause it all make sense. Take me far, I realise my instincts are real like it turns me on, some kind of magic runs through my

life. Every minute, I think this is the time of my life. Peaking, moving, it's good to be around again. A nice way to change everything. A nice way to change everything... Peaking, peaking, I'm having the time of my next turn. Could you see it coming? Where do we go from here? I don't want to stay the same. Could you see it coming? Where do we go from here? I guess we just missed 4 days. A feeling am I loosing my mind? Like a freefall

Like a freefall where I'm out of controll.

where I'm out of control. I'm shaking as I'm choking on my failure. Now I'm waiting for my next turn. Could you see it coming? Where do we go from here? I don't want to stay the same. Could you see it coming? Where do we go from here? I guess we just missed 4 days.

You are still a part of me.

I come back to see if you were here. It's nice to know you're well. Forgot the fact that I still care, so to you I've gained and I'm sane. Still I'm here with you. Still I'm here with you. Still I'm here with you. Still I'm here with you. Still I'm here with you. Still I'm here with you. Still I'm here with you.

SPYING FOR COSTAR

CoStar

ARE YOU A POEM OR ARE YOU JUST TRENDY?

VOLUME 1
ISSUE NO.1
JANUARY 2003

US $ / UK £ / EURO / NoK etc.
SEE YOUR LOCAL DEALER

INCLUDING 6 EXCITING NEW SONGS!
BROTHERS IN CRIME EP

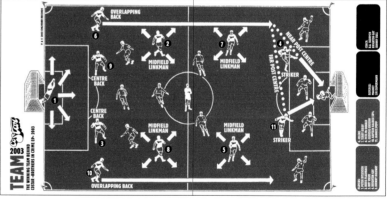

Design Martin Kvamme
Music   Co-Star
Format CD Cover, Book

- ROTATIONAL HIGH -

"TALK TO ME"

BLACK NOISE

MOGUAI
U KNOW Y

LABELCOPY

PUNX

KOSMO
RECORDS

Design	Io	Faktor
Music	Black Noise	Moguai
Format	CD Cover, Book	CD Cover

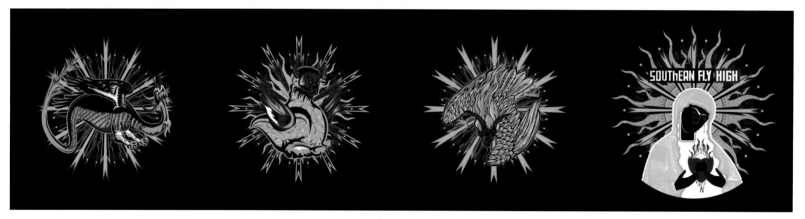

Design   Insect   Tsuyoshi Hirooka
Music   Southern Fly   Wanna Rock
Format   CD Covers, Books   Illustrations

SOUTHERN FLY MONKEY TALE

SOUTHERN FLY FOR REAL E.P.

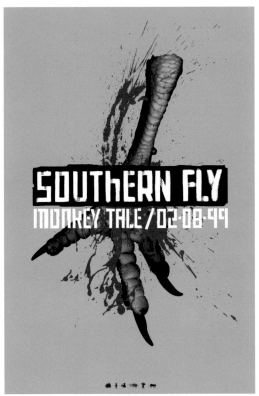

SOUTHERN FLY
MONKEY TALE / 02·08·99

SOUTHERN FLY
MAYBE IT'S THE RIGHT TIME
28·02·00

CD1. REMIX BY DOPE SMUGGLAZ CD2. REMIX BY FLIGHTCRANK
'MAYBE IT'S THE RIGHT TIME' TAKEN FROM THE FORTHCOMING ALBUM 'HIGH'

SOUTHERN FLY FOR REAL E.P.

SOUTHERN FLY MAYBE IT'S THE RIGHT TIME

SOUTHERN FLY MAYBE IT'S THE RIGHT TIME

173

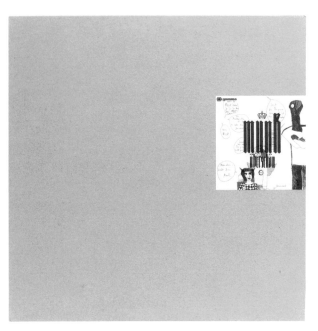

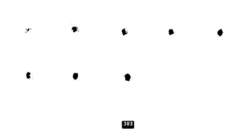

303

CD7FAT11
THE MUTTS

223

Design   Mirko Borsche   Fat Cat
Music   Munk   Various
Format   Vinyl Sleeves   CD Covers

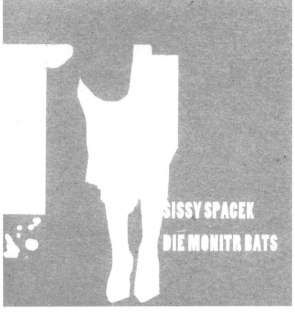

YOSHIO MACHIDA hypernatural # 2 1 Potential 2. Radiant Wind 3 Malaria 4 Afterimage 5 Valley 6 The Polar Lights 7 Deep Sound Channel 8 Daydream; all compositions by Yoshio Machida; track 4+5 composed by Yoshio Machida & Aki Onda; produced by Aki Onda; recorded by Yoshio Machida at Small Axe, Tokyo, april 2000; track 3 was recorded in Chiang Rai; track 2 +5 was recorded by Hideo Tanaka at the Kitchen, 2000, Tokyo; mixed by Yoshio Machida & Aki Onda at the Kitchen, Tokyo, may 2000; Pro Tools editing by Takehiko Kamata at the Border, Tokyo, 2000; Final Master by Tom Steinle at the Tomlab, Cologne 2001; *Yoshio Machida: field recordings, effects, vietnamese gong, kean pro2 metal cassette recorder, cassette recorder, mdo bamboo flute, wind, chimes, glasses, mouth harp, piano, SP 808; *Aki Onda: cassette recorder (track 4+6); *Saki: late deep sound organ (track 7); jacket design: frieda luczak; print: Knust; © by softlmusic; www.yoshiomachida.com; www.softlmusic.com

ALEJANDRA&AERON scotch monsters 1a. dunters 2b. each-uisge 3c. trows 4d. bluemen_ofthe_minch 5e. heather pixi 6f. fin folk 7g. nuckelavee 8h. brownie 9i. redcaps 10j. henkies 11k. boggie 12l. pixie 13m. baisd bheulach 14n. baisd bheulach 2 15o. fear liath more 16p. walking pow burn. Tracks 1a to 7l are water spirits. Tracks 8h to 16p are earth spirits. recordings made in stirling, glasgow, dollar glen, aloa, perthshire, clackmannanshire coast, pow burn, and a few unknown stops along the way: scotland. this is an audio revision of an audio revision from our install-ation: "revisionland" at the changing room, stirling, scotland (curated by diskono). the second revision became the bottrop-boy 12 inch, and this is the third and final rework. all information taken from the internet sites of scottish-american heritage aficionados. thanks to diskono, the changing room, the scottish arts council, kirsteen, robert, andres and tom, ultra red, xavier, jacob, s. mathieu, mark and angeline, "fallt" and our family. all tracks by alejandra and aeron except track 16 recorded by stuart mcgregor and katy dove, and edited by a & a. jacket design by f.luczak, extrapool and softl © by softlmusic, www.softlmusic.com

AKI ONDA precious moments 1 toward a place in the sun 2 the blank space 3 floating souls 4 caress 5 someplace 6 to and fro, entangling 7 orange 8 fish don't know it's raining 9 ravage 10 morning, june24 11 gazing into the eyes, then closing the eyes; all compositions by Aki Onda (JASRAC); except track 1 by Aki Onda (JASRAC) & Kazutoki Umezu (JASRAC); Aki Onda: cassette recorder, sampler, programming; Sakana Hosomi: electronics; Kazutoki Umezu: clarinet, slide whistle; Jyoji Sawada: acoustic guitar, kalimba; Momo: synthesizers; produced by Aki Onda; recorded by Aki Onda & Eiichi Tanaka at The Kitchen, Tokyo; mixed by ZAK at Storobo, Tokyo; assistant engineer: Yoshiki; jacket design: frieda Luczak; print: Knust; translation: Haruna Ito; © by softlmusic; www.akionda.com; www.softlmusic.com

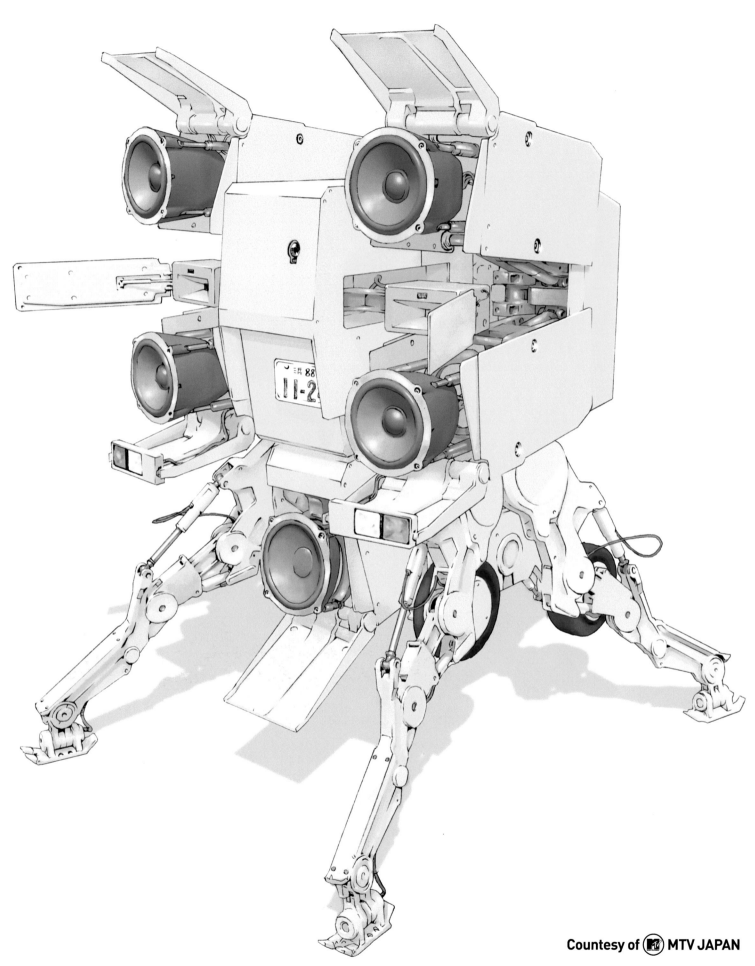

Design   Izmojuki
Music   MTV Japan
Format   Advertising

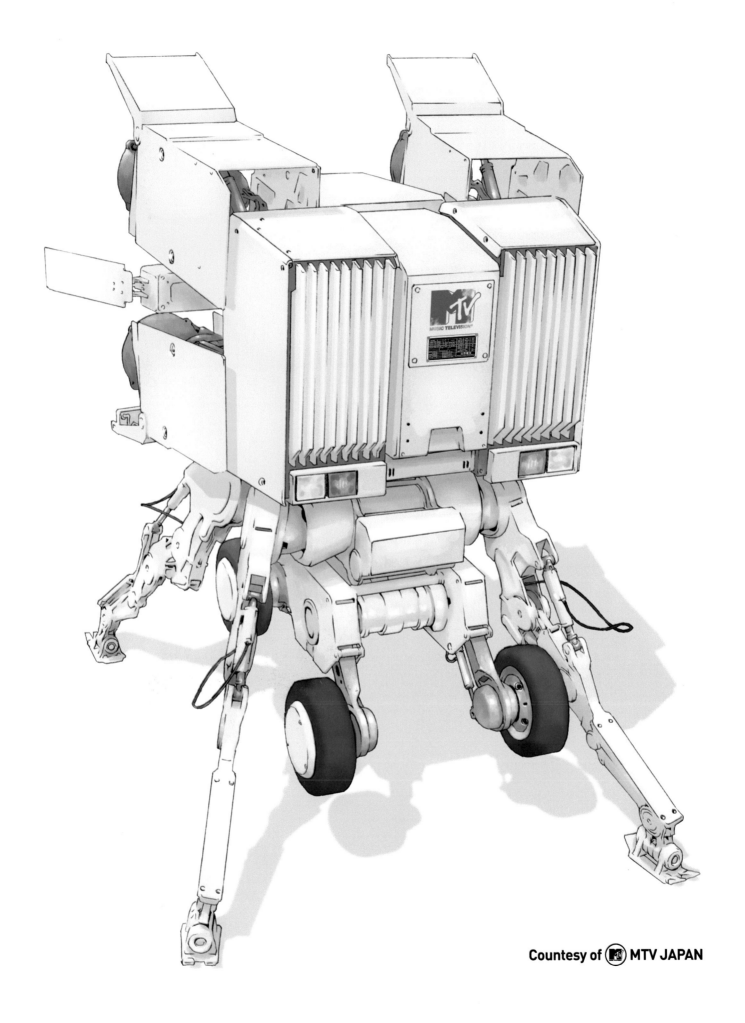

Countesy of MTV **MTV JAPAN**

Design   Foetus
Music   Foetus
Format   CD Covers

<s>andwich
thanks to the moon's gravitational pull

1. astroholiday
2. 2 trick pony
3. for your consideration
4. homerun
5. masilungan
6. nahuhulog
7. not this time
8. return to center
9. right now
10. scared shitless
11. surrounded by dogs
12. thanks to the moon

Design	Inksurge	Fons Hickmann
Music	Sandwich	Various
Format	CD Cover, Book	Poster Series

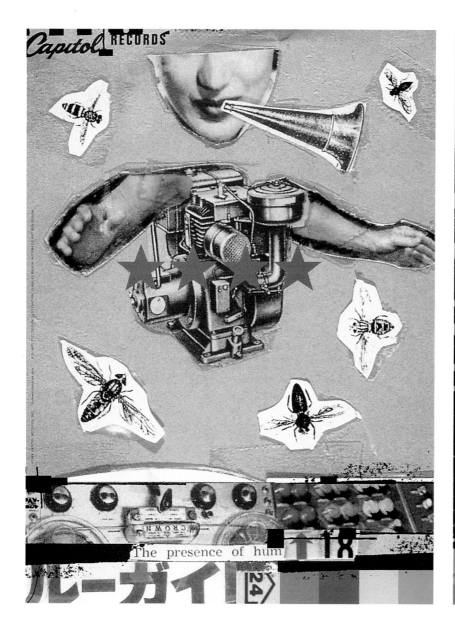

Design	Automatic	F27	Regina	Asterik
Music	The Presence of Hum, Screaming Cheetah Weelies	My Morning Jacket	Tone Flow	Joy Electric
Format	Ad, CD Covers	Gig Poster	CD Cover	CD Cover

THE UNIT
BIG
CHILL

MOVE ANY MOUNTAIN

THE UNIT
MOVE ANY
MOUNTAIN

INCOMMUNICADO

copenhagen jazz underground

LOST WAYS

FORBIDDEN FRUIT
LOST WAYS

Bindemittel

Design	Konstruktion	Quentaro "ANI" Fujimoto	Pfadfinderei
Music	The Unit, Copenhaven Jazz	Tanikugu	Bindemittel
Format	CD Covers, Flyers	CD Cover	CD Cover

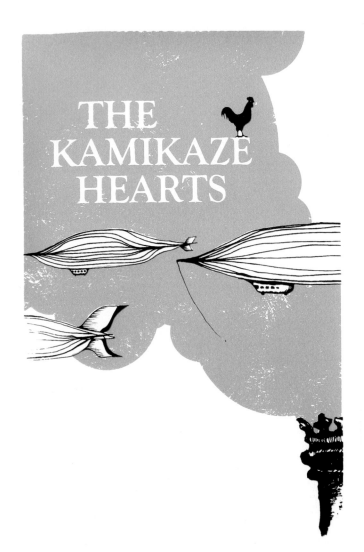

Design	Studio 1800	JDK
Music	The Kamikaze Hearts, Nakatomi Plaza	J. J. Cale
Format	Posters	Poster

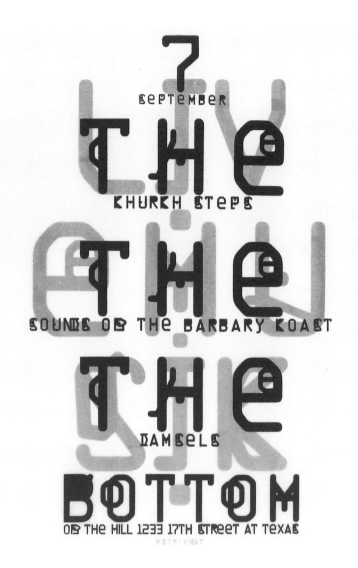

7 September

the
khurkh steps

the
sounds of the barbary koast

the
damsels

bottom
of the hill 1233 17th street at texas
petriknat

Design   Slang
Music   Various
Format   Gig Posters

ISOLATION YEARS
Frosted Minds

ISOLATION YEARS
It's Golden

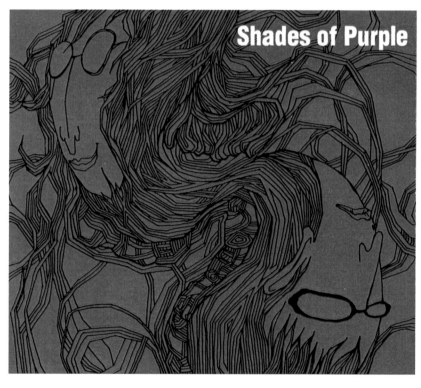

Shades of Purple

Design	Io	Tomoko Tsuneda
Music	Isolation Years	Dixied The Emons – Shades of Purple
Format	CD Covers	CD Cover

186

KRISTOFER ÅSTRÖM & HIDDEN TRUCK
CONNECTED

WITHOUT YOUR LOVE • YEARS SINCE YESTERDAY • GO, WENT, GONE • LEAVING SONG • THE OLD MAN'S MEADOW • ANOTHER TOWN

KRISTOFER ÅSTRÖM & HIDDEN TRUCK
NORTHERN BLUES

KRISTOFER ÅSTRÖM & HIDDEN TRUCK • PLASTERED CONFESSIONS

New Album!

Design   Jonas Banker
Music   Kristofer Åström
Format   CD Covers

Maximilian Hecker
Infinite Love Songs

Design   A.Lorenz
Music   Maximilian Hecker
Format   CD Covers

Maximilian Hecker **Polyester**

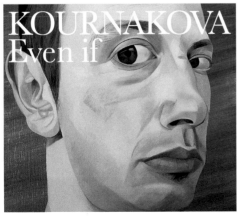

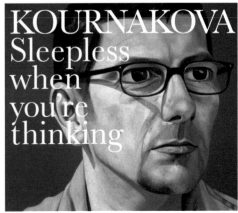

Design	Nick Havas/Justin Jones	Alternative Tentacles
Music	And Also The Trees	The Flaming Stars
Format	CD Covers	CD Covers

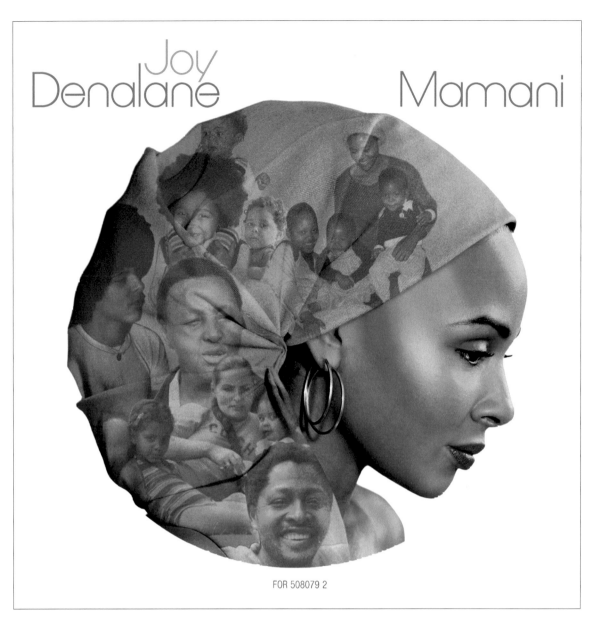

FOR 508079 2

Design   Disco Döner
Music   Joy Denalane, Freundeskreis
Format   CD Covers

Design	Zion	Methane
Music	Home Sweet House Compilation	Stereolab
Format	CD Cover	Gig Poster

FROZEN HAWAII
bonjour hawaii remixes
seasoning by Pardon Kimura

Felicidade
A Tribute to João Gilberto

AMERICAN RAG CIE Presents
The Wedding Project

Design   Enlightenment
Music   Various (Frozen Hawaii, Tribute to João Gilberto, Tsuki No Wa, The Wedding Project)
Format   CD Covers

Design Victoria Collier
Music Mojave 3
Format CD Cover

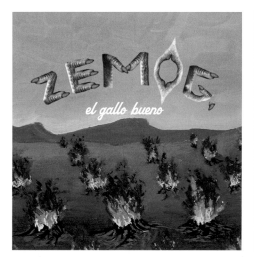

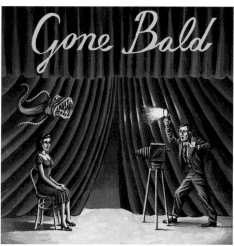

Design   Jan Lankisch   FJD   Honest   Laura Varsky   Interstellar
Music   Compilation   The Returning Sun, Doggy Style, A.D.M., Calm   Zemog   La Zurda   Gone Bald
Format   CD Cover   CD Covers   CD Cover   CD Cover   CD Cover

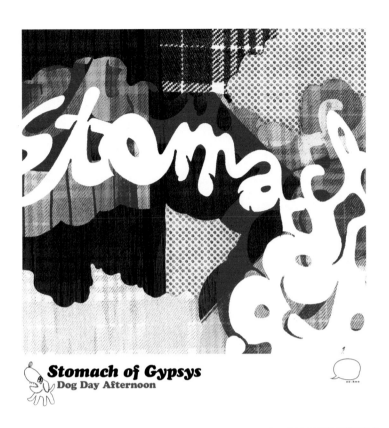

Stomach of Gypsys
Dog Day Afternoon

Design   FJD
Music   Stomach of Gypsys, Golf, Loversrock
Format   Flyers

Design	Insect
Music	House of Wax, Jack Planck
Format	CD Cover

198

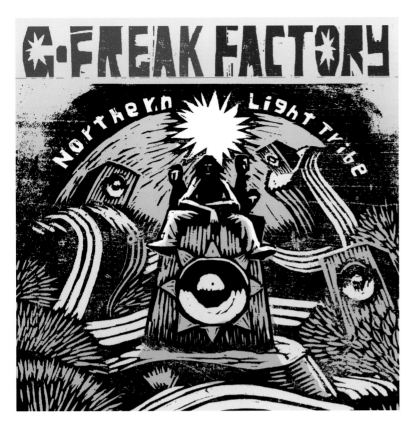

Design   2Yang
Music   G-Freak Factory, Various Artists / Blue Frame Dub
Format   CD Covers

Design   Stephan Doitschinoff
Music   Saves the Day
Format   CD Cover, Book

Design   Tomoko Tsuneda
Music   Aco, Dixied The Emons
Format   CD Covers

ACO absolute live 2000

Design   Tomoko Tsuneda
Music   Aco
Format   Sticker, Video Packaging

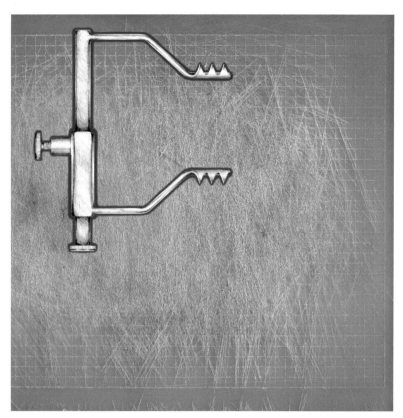

Floor-Tiling Project

Design   Eh?
Music   Various
Format   Vinyl Sleeves

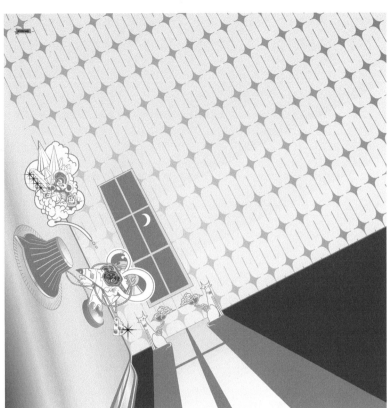

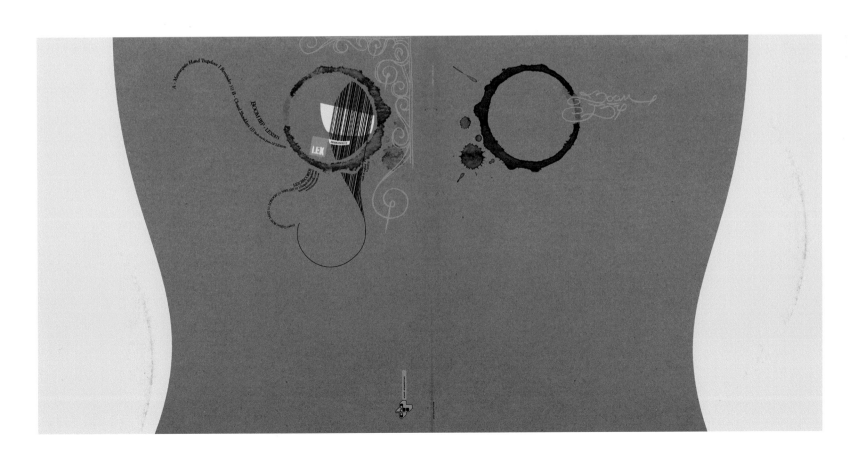

PILOT BALLOON
ghastly good cheer

kaospilot
debut lp/cd available june 9th

kaoSpiLot

level-plane

Design	SFausting	Regina
Music	Pilot Balloon	Kaospilot
Format	CD Cover	CD Cover, Ad

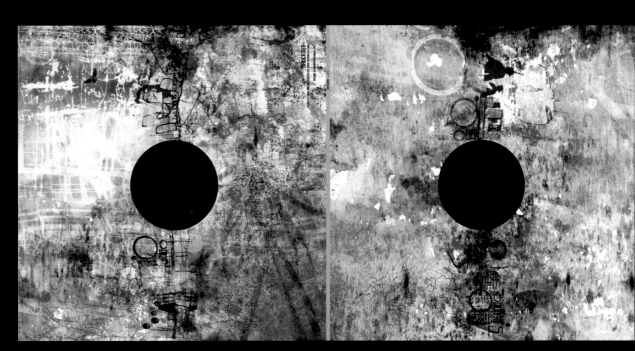

Katsumi Yokota Knat FM

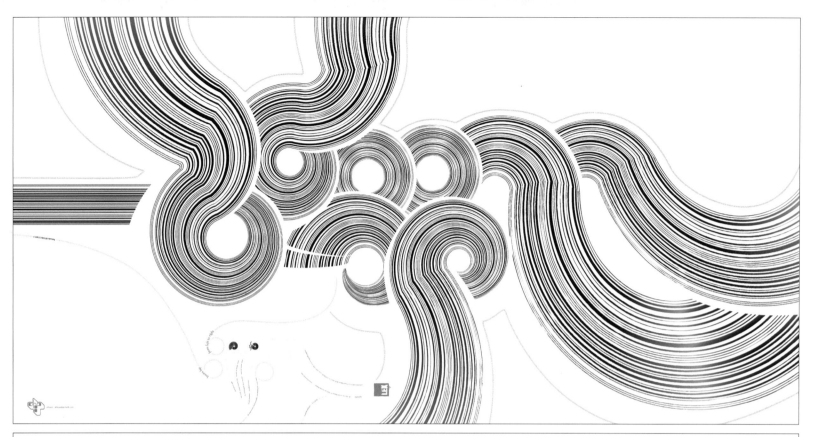

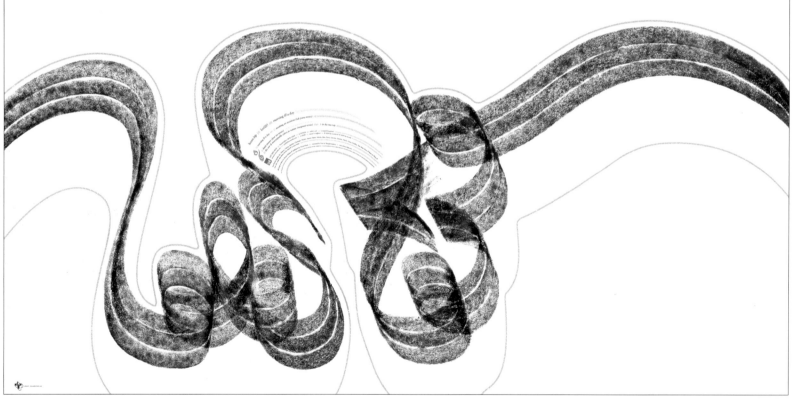

Design   Eh?
Music   Boom Bip
Format   Vinyl Sleeves

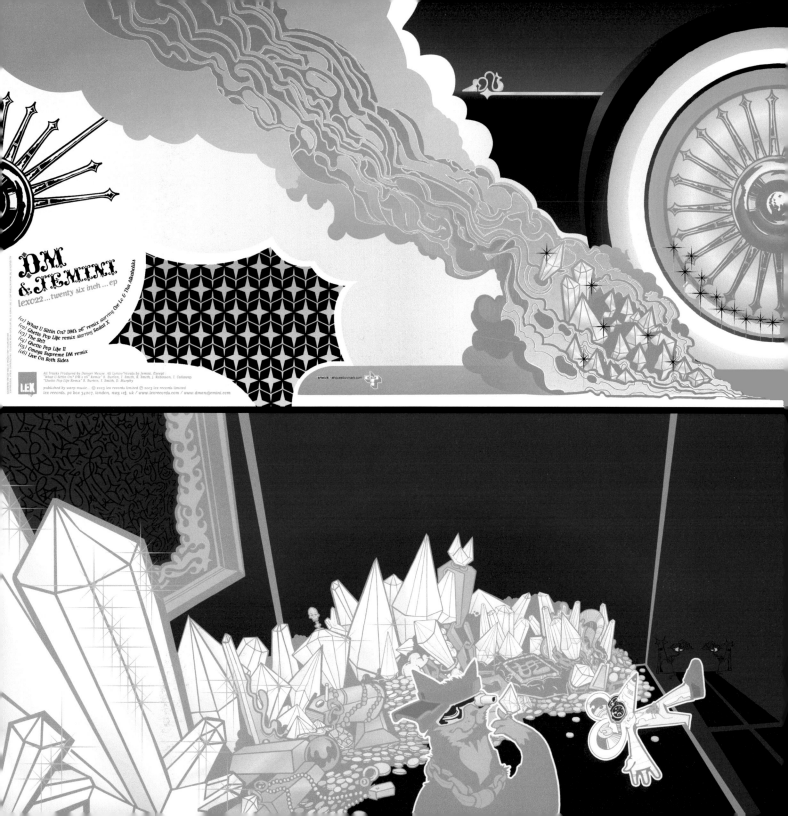

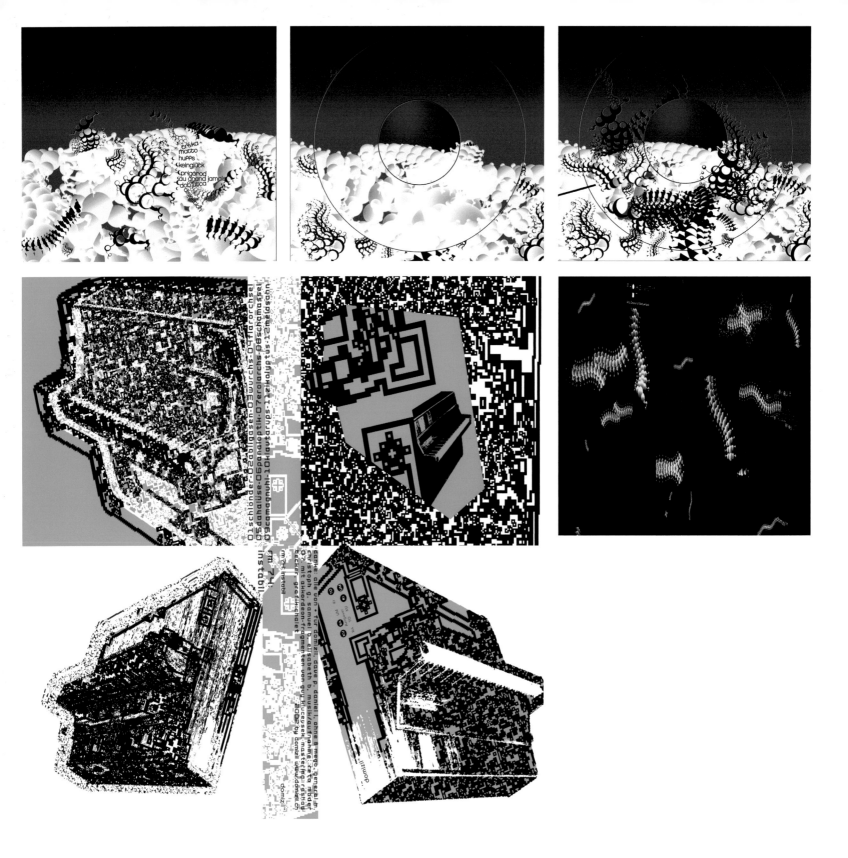

Design   François Chalet
Music   Various
Format   CD Covers

 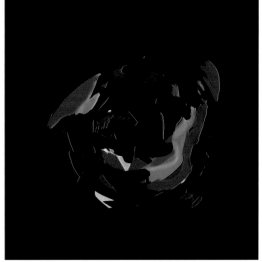 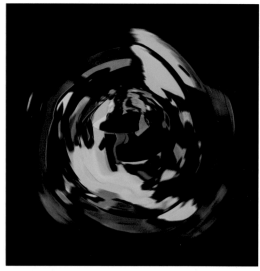

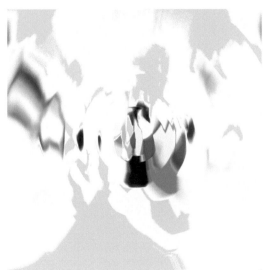 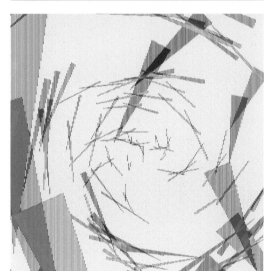 

 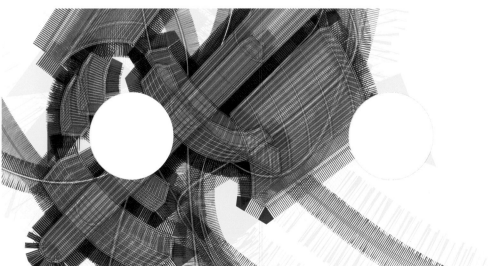

Design	Hideki Inaba	Christoph Leidig	Bowling Club
Music	RE: MOVEMENT	Iont	Idei Lahesna
Format	CD Book, Booklet	Single Sleeve	Vinyl Sleeve

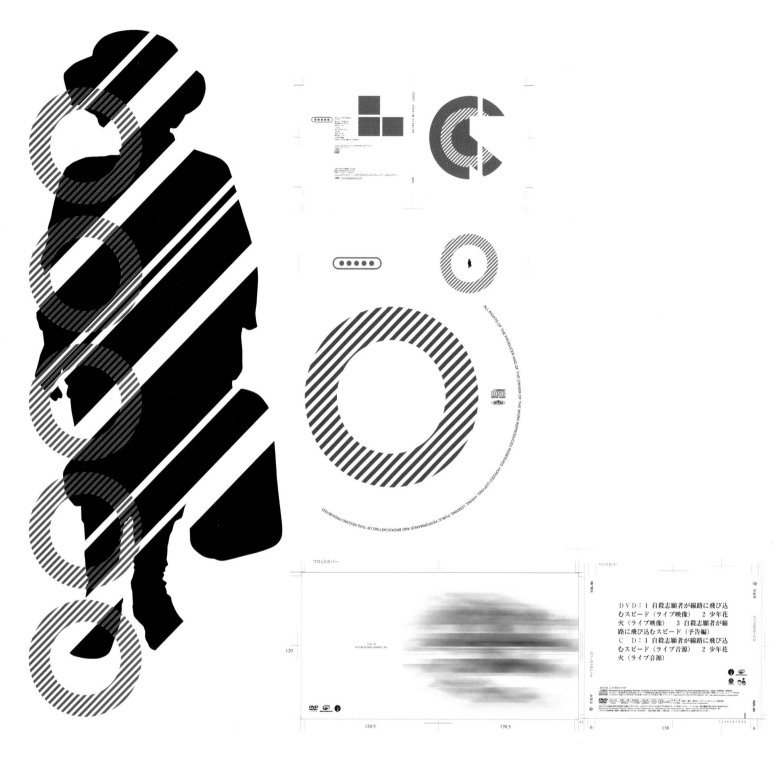

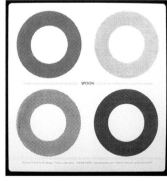

Design　　Tsuyoshi Kusano　　F27
Music　　　5rb　　　　　　　　Spoon
Format　　CD Covers　　　　　Gig Posters

THIS IS THE MONKEY
ODE TO JOY

WARM CIRCUIT ®   WARM001   WWW.WARMCIRCUIT.COM

Design   Lessrain
Music   Modified Toy Orchestra
Format   Single Sleeve

Design   Rune Mortensen
Music   Martin Horntveth, Paal Nilssen-Love/Håkon Kornstad
Format   CD Covers

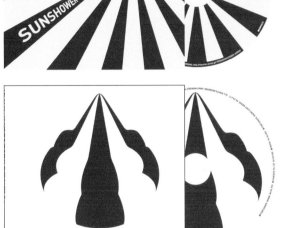

KEV
LAR

LE™ƐWORRY SOMEMOre

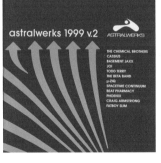

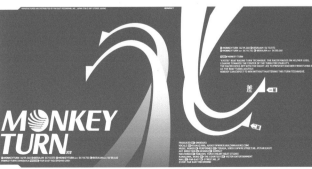

Design	Robert Samsonowitz	Quentano "ANI" Fujimoto	Nobody	Honest
Music	Kevlar	Sunshower, Fortunate 1Mark, Monkey Turn	Sing like Talking	Astralwerks Compilation
Format	Vinyl Sleeve	CD Covers	CD Covers	CD Cover

215

hed kandi

Fuel
Do 4 Love

HED

do 4 ♥

Design   Zip
Band   Fuel, Lazy Grace
Format   Vinyl Sleeves

Lazy Grace feat Billie Godfrey
How Deep Is Your Love

StoneBridge Club Mix
Lazy Grace Original 12" Mix
Johnny Fiasco's Deep Function Mix

City Approach
3am Gherkin

grandadbob

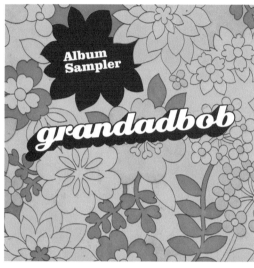

Album
Sampler

grandadbob

Secret
Tracks

grandadbob

Maybe

grandadbob

Waltzes For
Glastonbury

Waltzes For Weirdoes
Full Length Album Release
August 11th 2003.

grandadbob

Design   Zip
Music   Grandadbob
Format   CD Covers

Design   Klon
Music   Marvellous
Format   CD Cover

Design	Sweden	Mirko Borsche
Music	Quantic, Dr. Kosmos	Leroy Hang Hofer
Format	CD Covers	CD Book

Some of the items for the annual summer concert *"Jamboree99"*, sponsored by Chicago radio station, Q101.
They included everything from posters to individual band comic books, passes, t-shirts, stage design and much more.

Design   Carlos Segura
Music   Various
Format   Comics

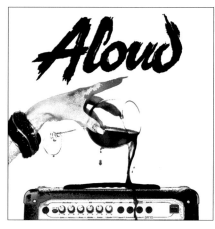

Design   Big Active
Music   A, Aloud
Format   CD Covers

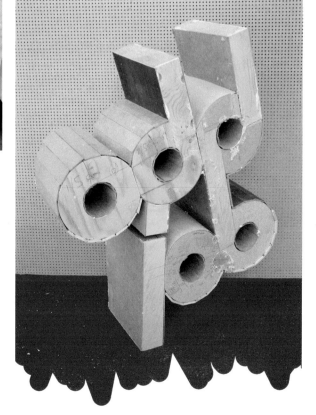

Design   Sweden   Dan Abbott
Music   Odd Job, Komeda   On Trial
Format   CD Covers   CD Cover

223

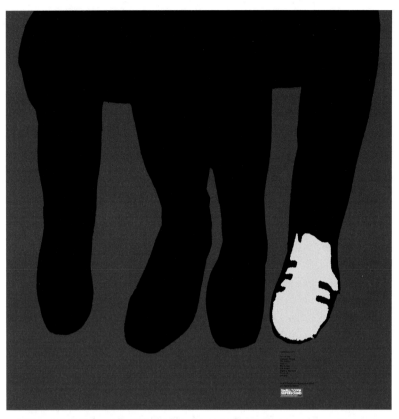

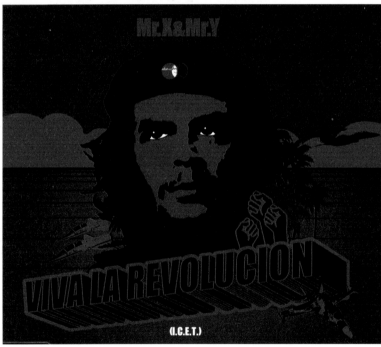

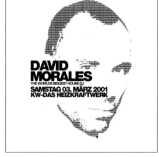

Design	Kim Hiorthøy	Disko Döner	Faktor	National Forest	Büro Destruct
Music	Midnight drummer	Mr.X & Mr.Y	Bob Dylan, David Morales	Al Green	Alphatronic
Format	Vinyl Sleeve	CD Cover	CD Cover, Flyer	CD Cover	Flyer

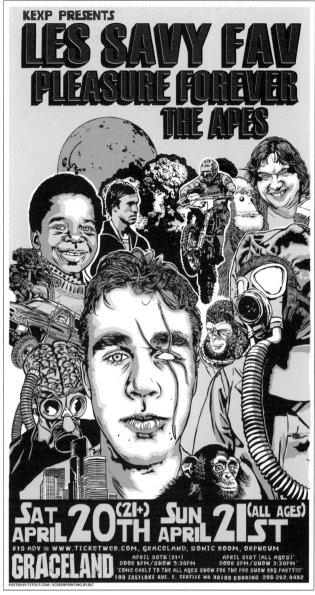

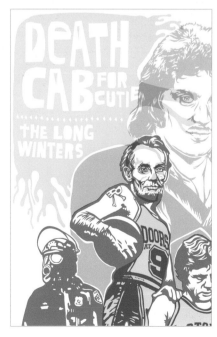

Design
Music
Format

T. Stout
Ex-Best Friend, Les Savy Fav, Death Cab for Cutie
Gig Posters

Superlow
Black Low
Poster

National Forest
Ubiquity
Poster

225

Design	NonFormat	Quentaro "ANI" Fujimoto
Music	Connectors	Back In The S.S.T. Band!! −The Very Best −
Format	Poster, Vinyl Sleeve	CD Cover

Design   Martin Kvamme
Music   Fantômas, Tomahawk
Format   Gig Poster, Tour Poster

228

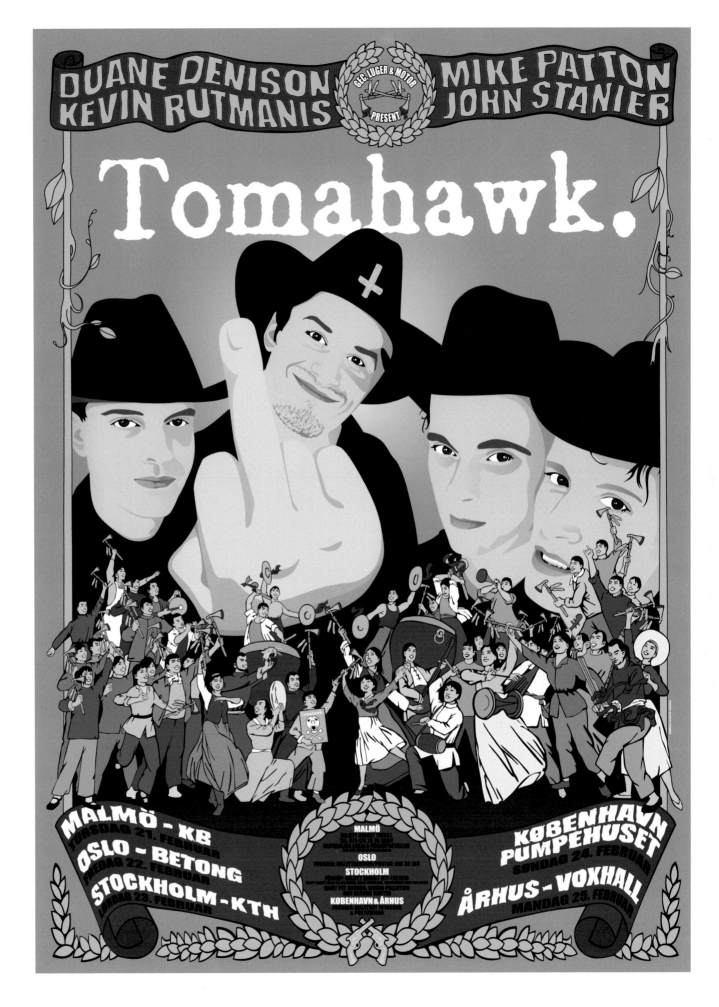

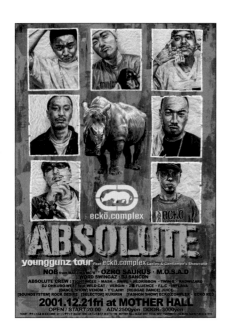

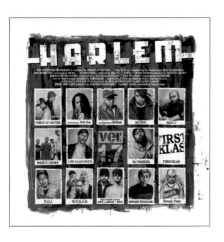

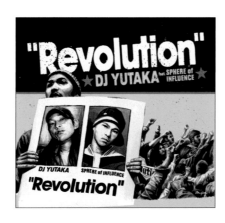

Design   Dragon
Music   Various
Format   Gig/Promotion Posters, Flyer, CD Covers

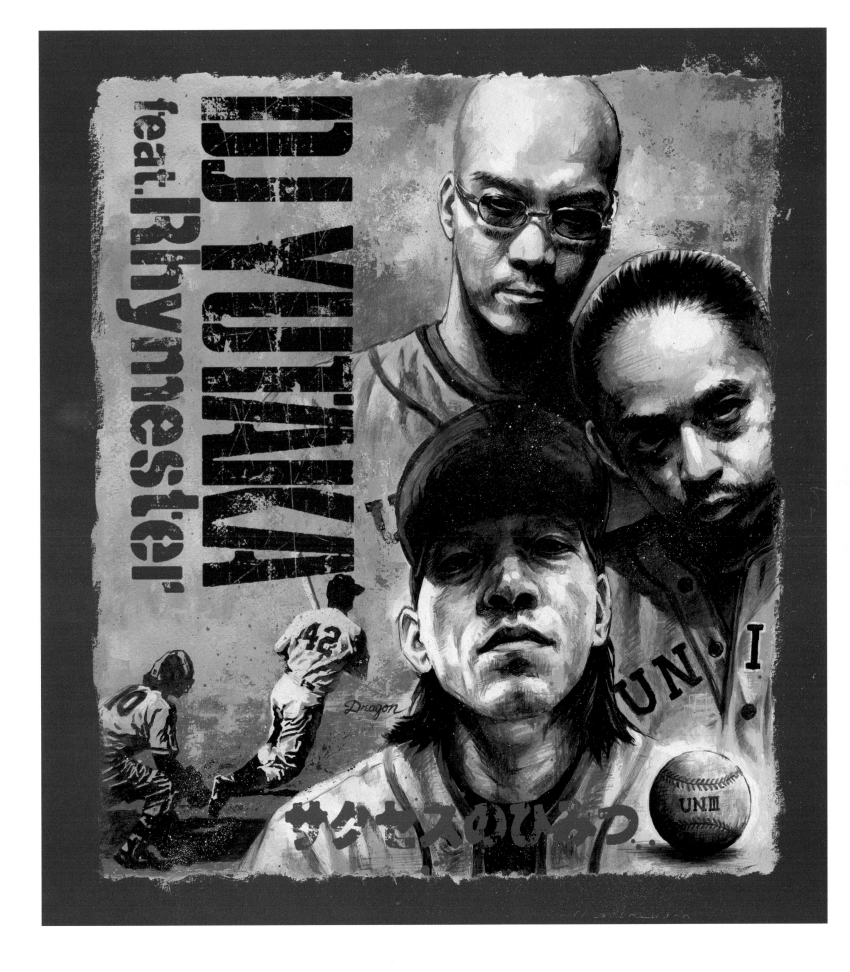

231

Design	Rockin' Jelly Bean
Music	The Flamenco A Go Go, The 5.6.7.8's
Format	CD/Vinyl Covers

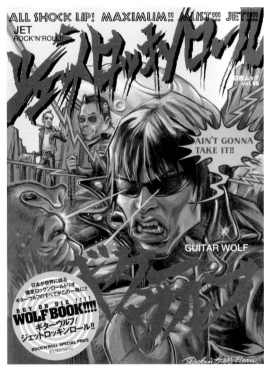

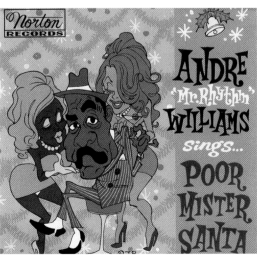

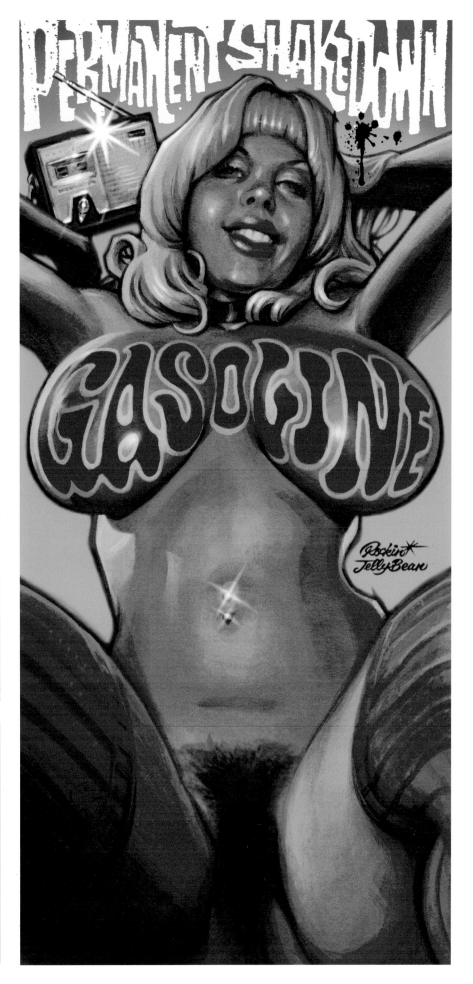

Design   Rockin' Jelly Bean
Music   Guitar Wolf, Andre Williams, Gasoline
Format   Book Cover, 7"ep Cover, CD Cover

Design   Red   Scumbucket
Music   Piss   Scumbucket
Format   Picture Disk Picture Disk

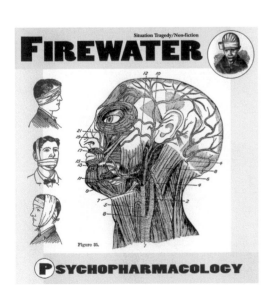

Design	Dragon	Io	Alternative Tentacles	Sweden	Firewater	Mother Tongue
Music	New York Times - Various	Caesars Palace, Dungen	Lard	The Raveonettes	Firewater	Mother Tongue
Format	CD Cover	CD Cover	CD Cover	CD Cover	CD Cover	CD Cover

235

Design	Martin Kvamme	Airside	Benjamin Güdel	2Yang
Music	Kaada	People in Planes	Deliquent Habits, David Bowie, True Colors	Various "Japanese Renaissance"
Format	Poster	Poster	Posters	Gig Poster

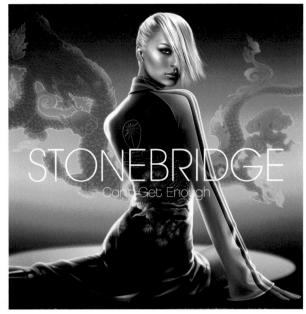

Design	Brainbox	Zip	Tsuyoshi Hirooka	K7
Music	Kamino	Stonebridge, Cosmos	Capsule, Golden Christmas	Mas
Format	CD Cover	CD Covers	CD Covers	CD Cover

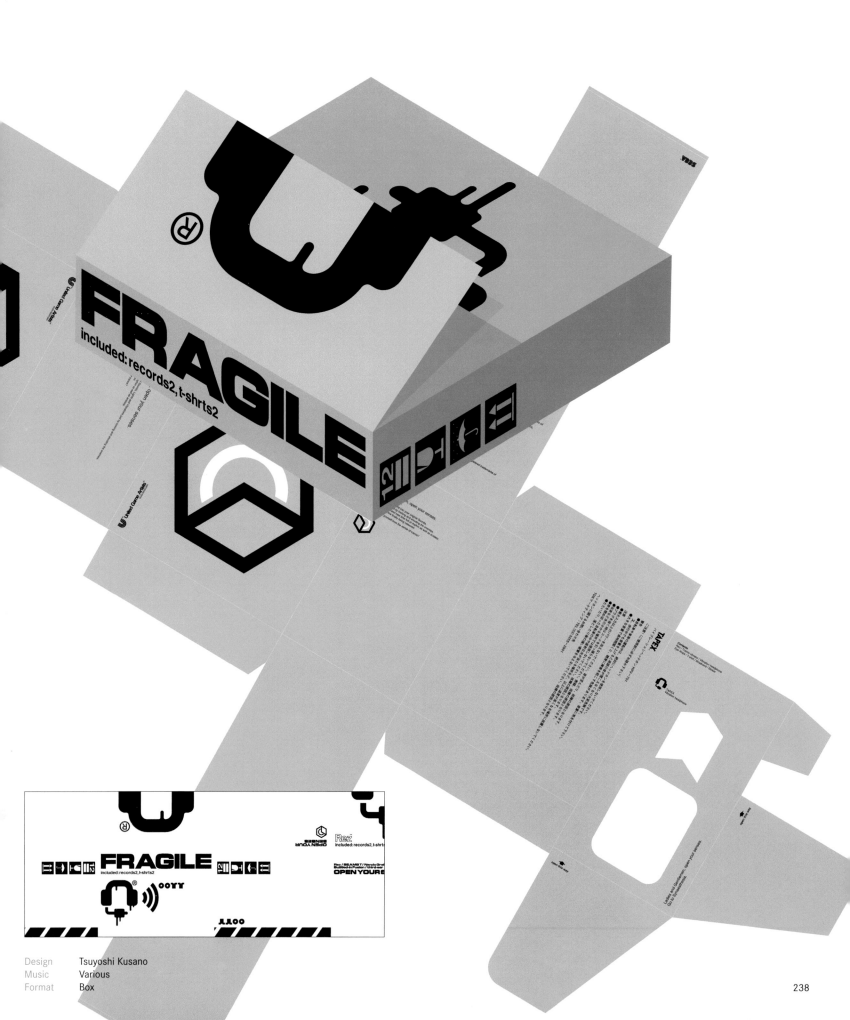

Design   Tsuyoshi Kusano
Music   Various
Format   Box

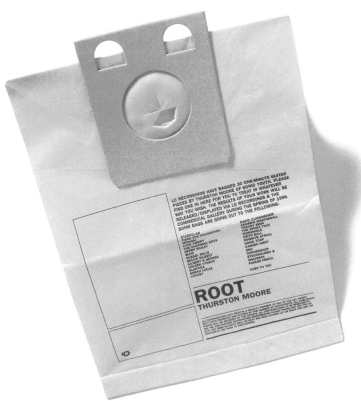

Design   NonFormat
Music   Root Project Thurston Moore
Format   CD Packaging

239

Design   Airside
Music   Various
Format   CD Packaging

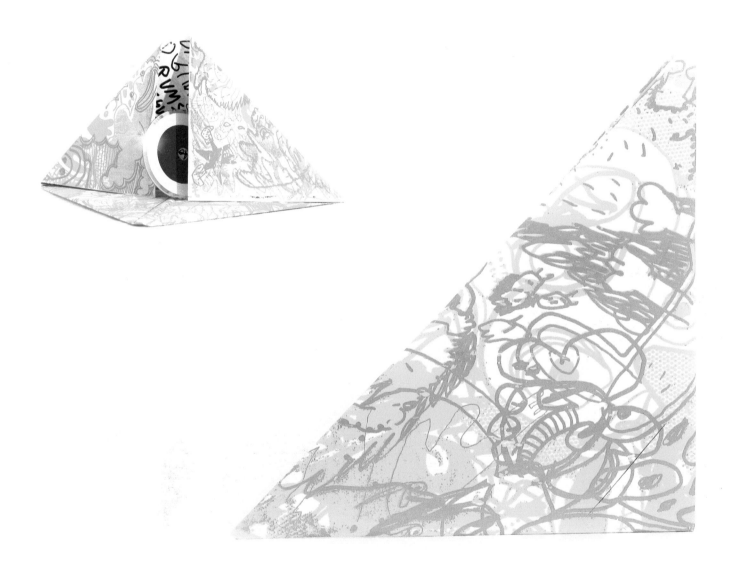

Design   Dennis Tyfus
Music   The Womups
Format   CD Packaging

Design	Manfred Engelmayr
Music	Bulbul
Format	CD Packaging

Design   Tom Hulan   Manfred Engelmayr, Tom Hulan
Music   Bulbul   Bulbul
Format   CD Packaging Feather   CD Packaging Velo

Design   Charhizma / d+ / various illustrators
Music   Charhizma Compilation Project "Platte"
Format   Special Vinyl Packaging (with fake picture disks)

244

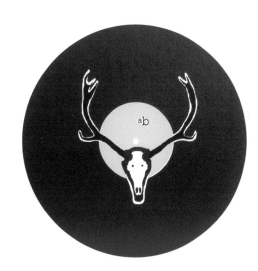

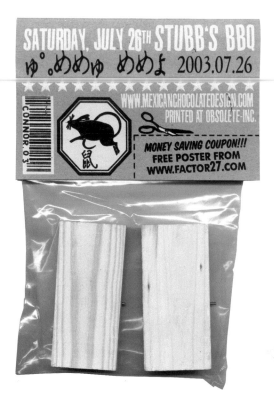

Design	Charhizma / d+	Jared Connor
Music	Orchester 33 1/3	Modest Mouse
Format	Special CD Packaging (out of old records)	Special Flyer/ Poster

246

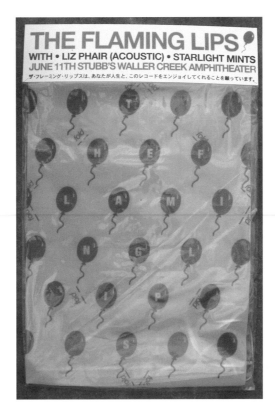
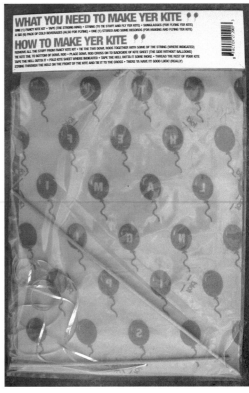

Bikini Wax
DJ Mary Mary & DJ Aleks Duplee
We Got Beef, Iso Roobertinkatu 21, Hki
Perjantai 88.88

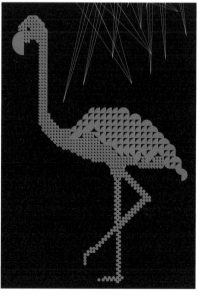

Bikini Wax
DJ Mary Mary & DJ Aleks Duplee
We Got Beef, Iso Roobertinkatu 21, Hki
Perjantai 88.88

Wax Off   **Wax On**   **Bikini Wax**

Design   Mongrel
Music   Bikini Wax
Format   Poster

THE CHAP
THE HORSE

****
LCD36/LLP36

****
Album out now
****
www.lorecordings.com
www.thechap.org

Design   NonFormat
Music   The Chap
Format   Poster, CD Cover

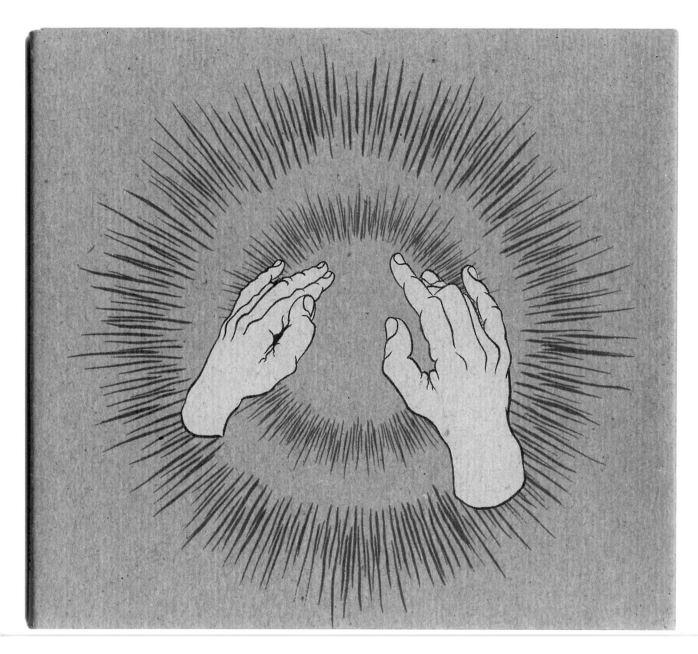

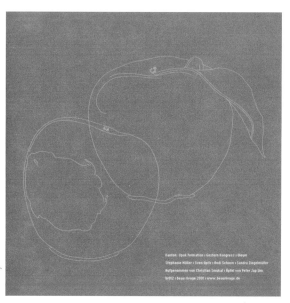

Design	Godspeed You Black Emperor	Christoph Leidig / Louise Clarke	Peter Jap Lim
Music	Godspeed You Black Emperor	State River Widening	Kanton
Format	CD Cover	Single Sleeve	Single Sleeve

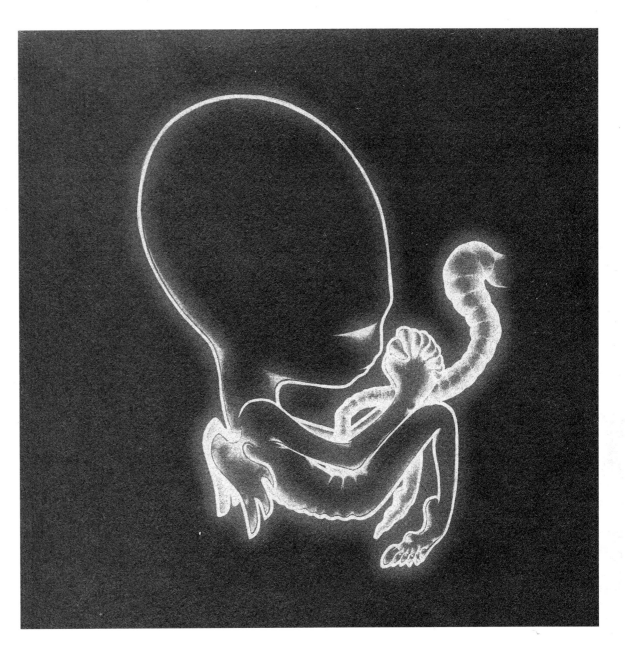

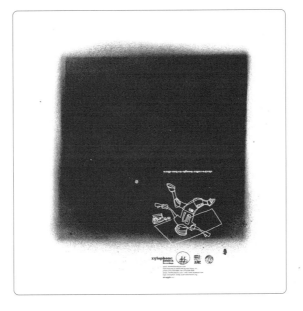

Design Agust Æevar Gunnarsson Struggle
Music Sigur Ros Electro-Roller-Boogie-Techno-Disco
Format CD Cover Vinyl Sleeve

Design   Zion
Music   Thomas Rusiak
Format   CD Cover, Book

Design   Studio 1800
Music   The Brian Jonestown Massacre
Format   Poster

Design	Insect	Superlow	Surface
Music	Savile Robots	Thorns	Shantel
Format	Vinyl Sleeve	CD Cover	CD Cover

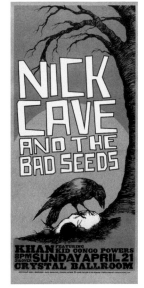

Design	Heads of State	Shrine	Mike King	Rocking Jelly Bean
Music	Bonnie Prince Billy	Flora Reed	Nick Cave, Ben Harper	Let's get back...
Format	Gig Poster	Gig Poster	Gig Posters	Gig Poster

255

Design   Asterik
Music   Various
Format   Tour Poster

THOMAS RUSIAK | UNICORN

5050466-4383-5-5

01. UNICORN | 3:31 | 02. UNICORN INSTRUMENTAL | 3:31 | 03. SPINNING VIDEO | 4:16 |

WRITTEN & ARRANGED BY THOMAS K. RUSIAK. CO. WRITTEN & CO. ARRANGED BY S.K. RUSIAK.

Design   Zion
Music   Thomas Rusiak
Format   CD Cover

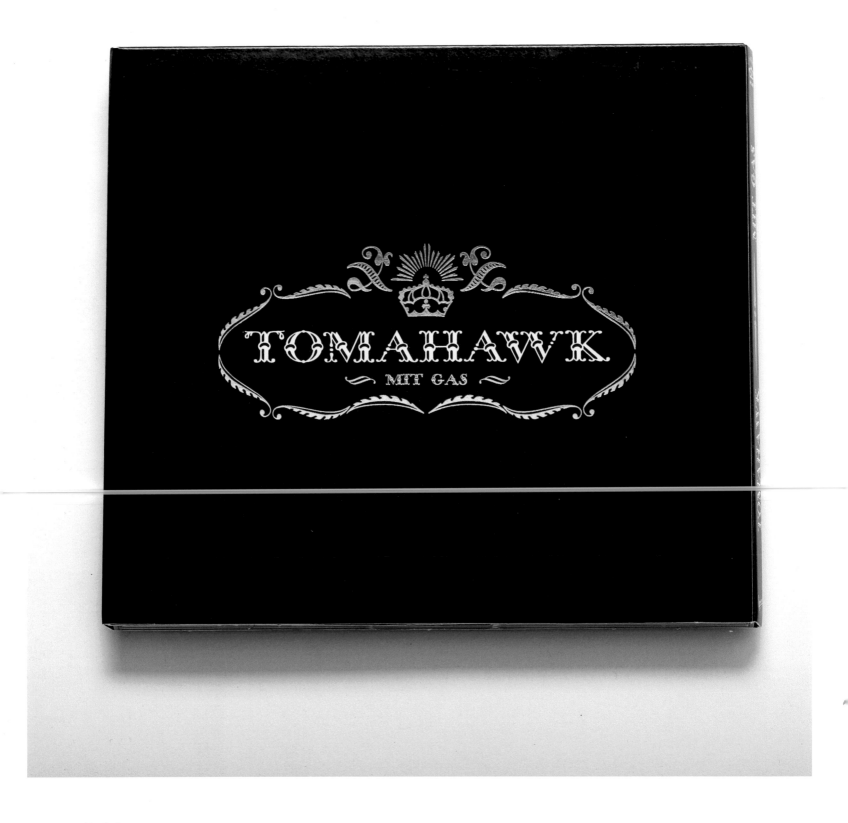

Design   Martin Kvamme
Music   Tomahawk
Format   CD Cover

Design   Usugrow
Music   Evil C
Format   Poster

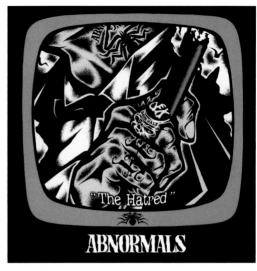

Design   Usugrow
Music   Evil C, Abnormals, Beast Feast, Shadows Fall, Various
Format   CD Covers, Gig Posters

Design   Superlow
Music   Satyricon
Format   Vinyl Sleeve, Poster

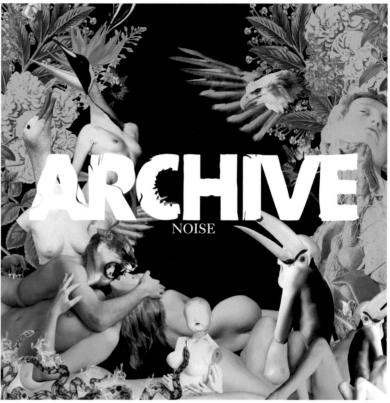

Design   Insect
Music   Archive
Format   CD Covers

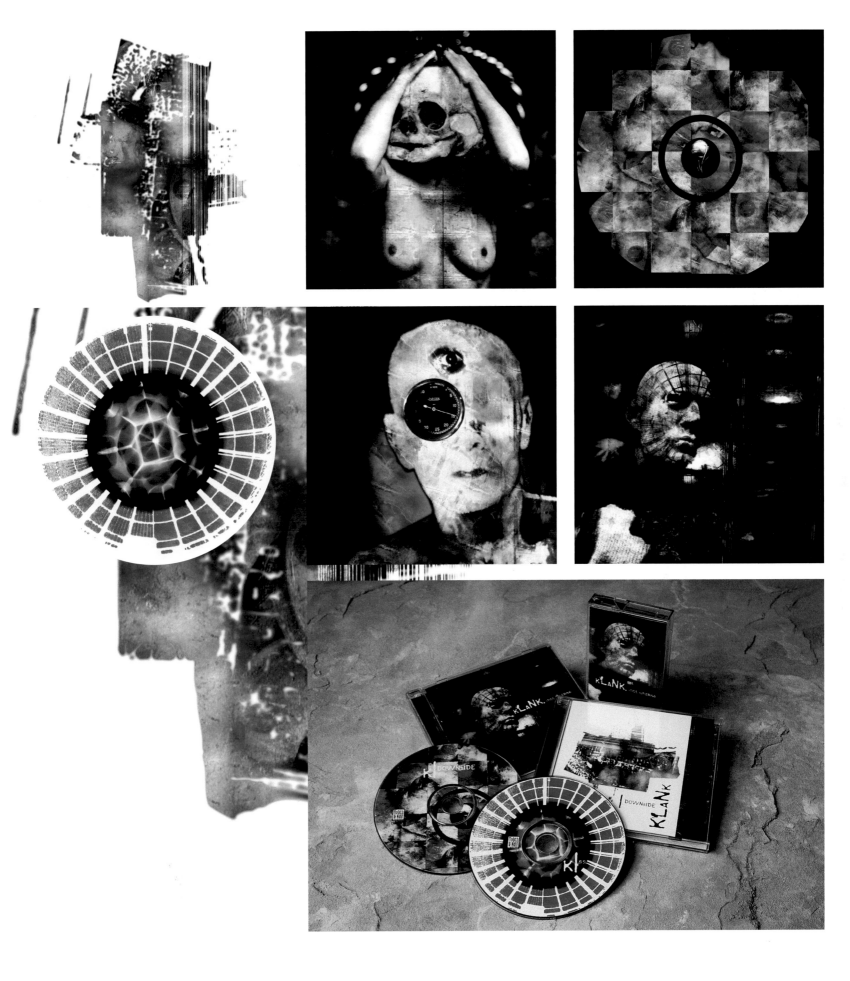

Design   Carlos Segura
Music   Various
Format   CD Covers

Design   Dirk Rudolph
Music   Covenant, De/Vision
Format   CD Covers, Books

268

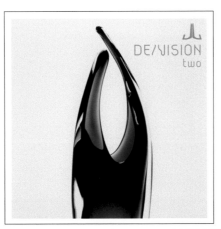

Design   Dirk Rudolph
Music   In Extremo, Ilse DeLange
Format   CD Covers, Books

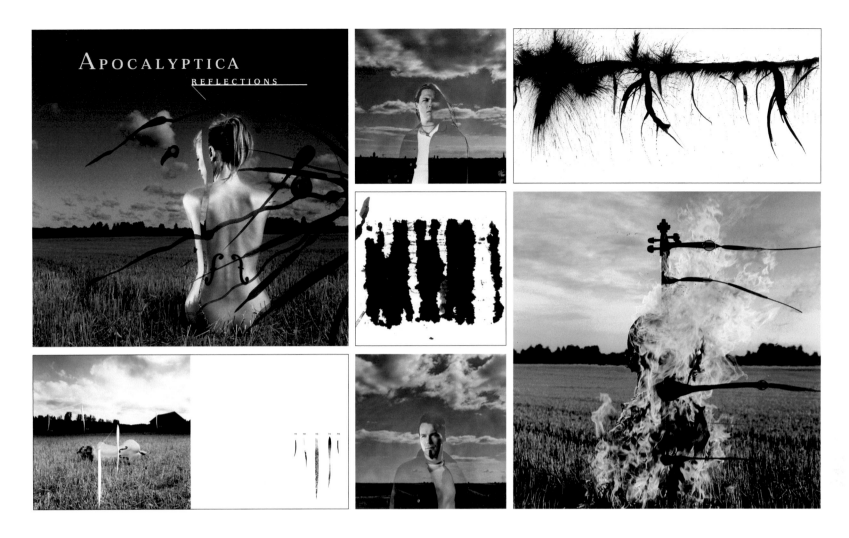

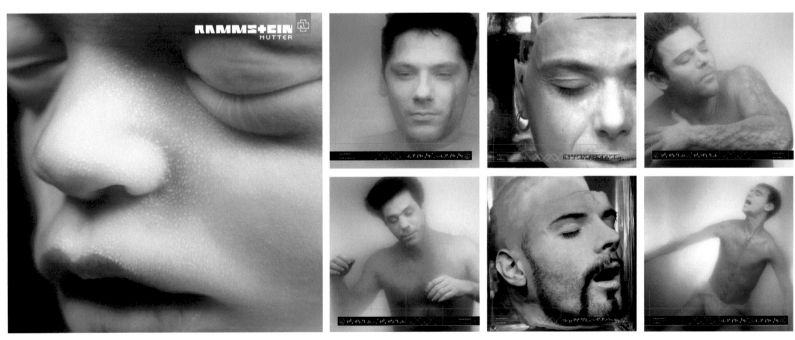

Design   Dirk Rudolph
Music   Apocalyptica, Rammstein
Format   CD Covers, Books

IN EXTREMO
Unter dem Meer

IN EXTREMO
LIMITED EDITION
COLLECTORS BOX SET

Design   Dirk Rudolph
Music   In Extremo
Format   CD Covers

PIA LUND

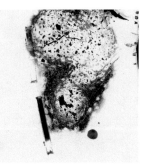

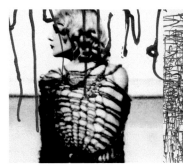

Design	Dirk Rudolph
Music	Pia Lund
Format	CD Covers

Design   Stylorouge
Music   Halo
Format   CD Cover

SYNTAX
MECCANO
MIND

Design   Big Active
Music   Syntax
Format   CD Cover

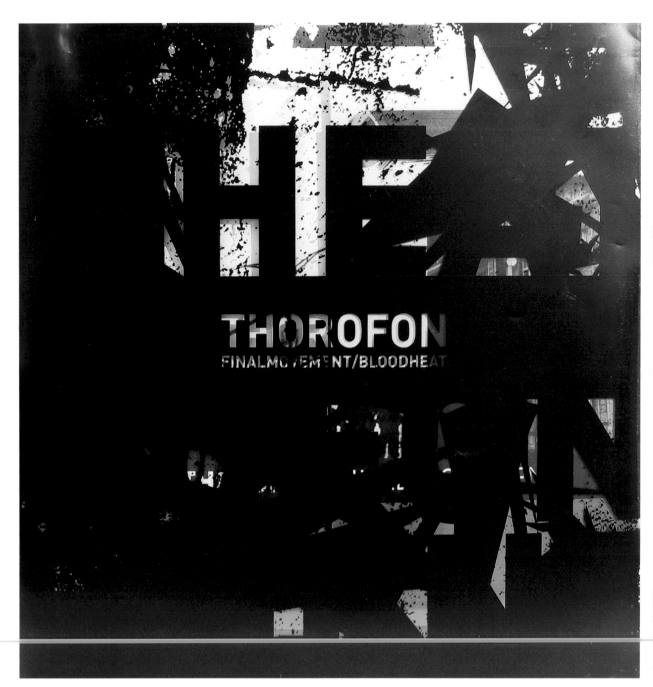

the fact that
we no longer
accept their
system makes
them nervous...
...and that's exactly what we want!

bloodheat
THOROFON

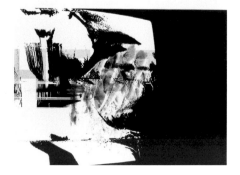

Design   Blind Research
Music   Thorofon
Format   Vinyl Sleeves

Design   Dirk Rudolph
Music   Rammstein
Format   DVD Cover

blackmail
friend or foe?

Design   Dirk Rudolph
Music   Blackmail
Format   CD Covers

blackmail
foe

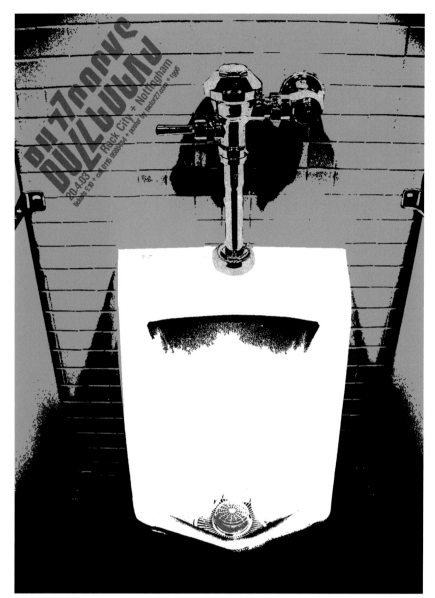

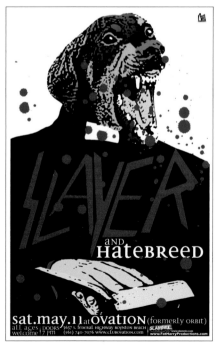

Design	F 27	Jared Connor	Chuck Loose
Music	Buzzcocks	Jon Spencer Blues Explosion	Slayer
Format	Gig Poster	Gig Poster	Gig Poster

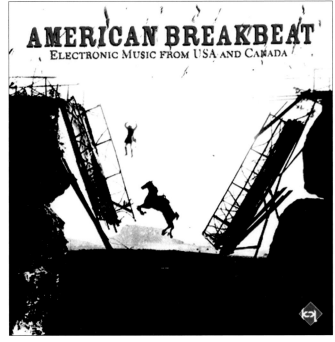

Design	Jared Connor	Zion	Klangkrieg
Music	Social Distortion	The Faint, Radio 4	American Breakbeat Compilation
Format	Gig Poster	Gig Poster	CD Covers

281

ALL PHOTOS BY MAX AGUILERA-HELLWEG © 1997

TAKEN FROM THE BOOK «THE SACRED HEART» · BVLLFINCH PRESS
VSED BY PERMISSION

IV · tumor associated with liver disease

Design	Martin Kvamme
Music	Fantomas
Format	CD Cover, Booklet

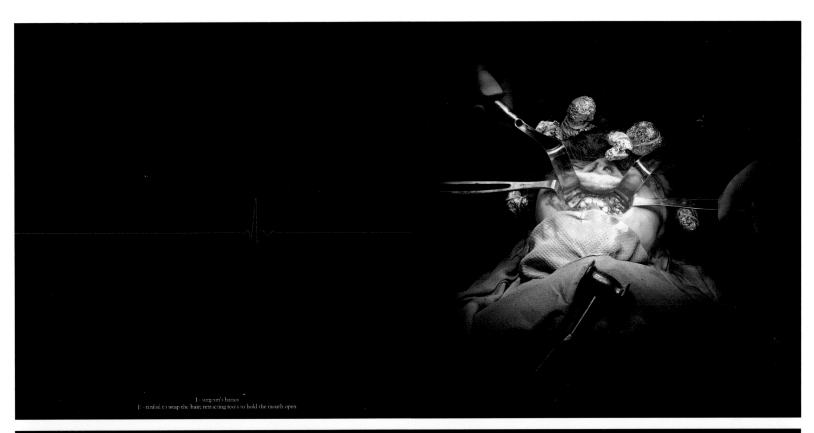

I - surgeon's hands
I - tinfoil to wrap the hair; retracting tools to hold the mouth open

V - organ donation for cornea transplant

Design   Martin Kvamme
Music   Gluecifer
Format   CD Cover, Booklet

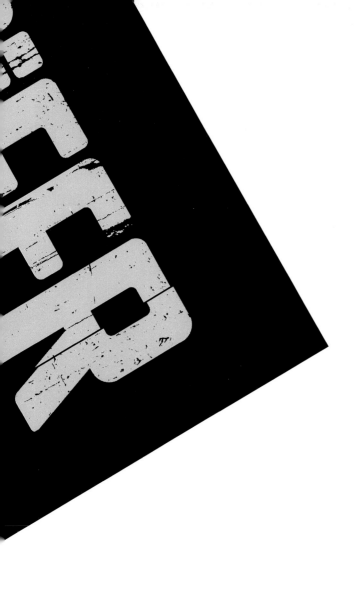

Design   Robert Samsonowitz
Music   The New Mess
Format   CD Cover, Booklet

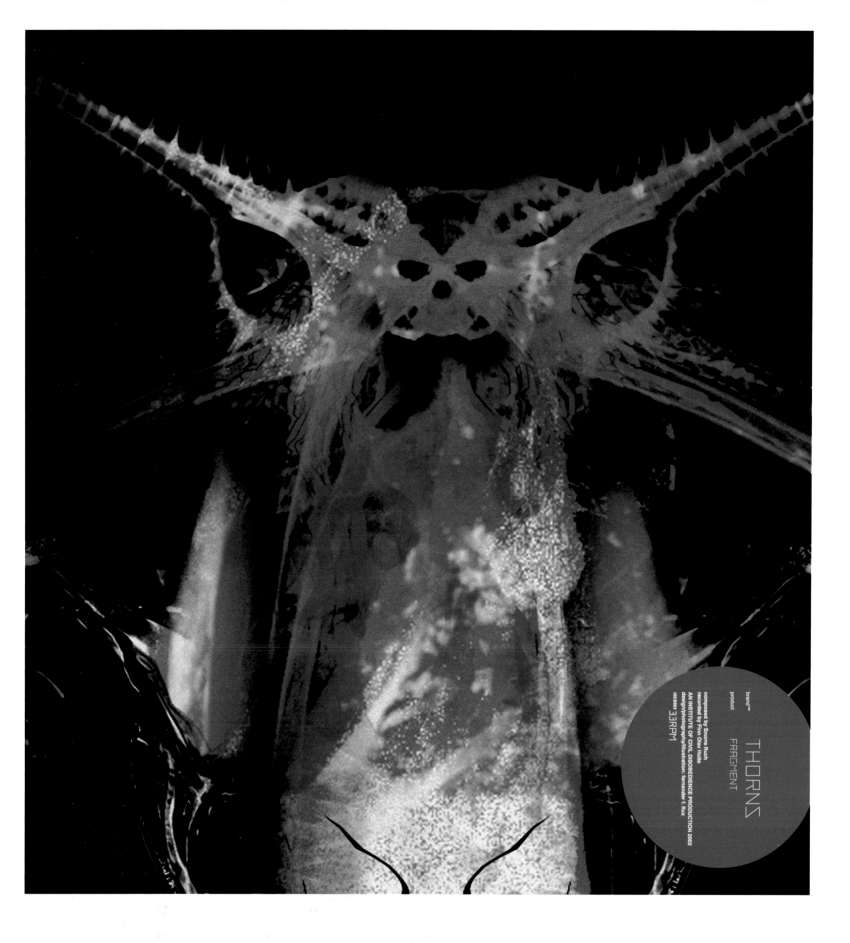

brand™
product

THORNS
FRAGMENT

composed by Snorre Ruch
recorded by Finn Olav Holle
AN INSTITUTE OF CIVIL DISOBEDIENCE PRODUCTION 2002
design/photography/illustration: fernandez f. flux
iicasa₂ 33RPM

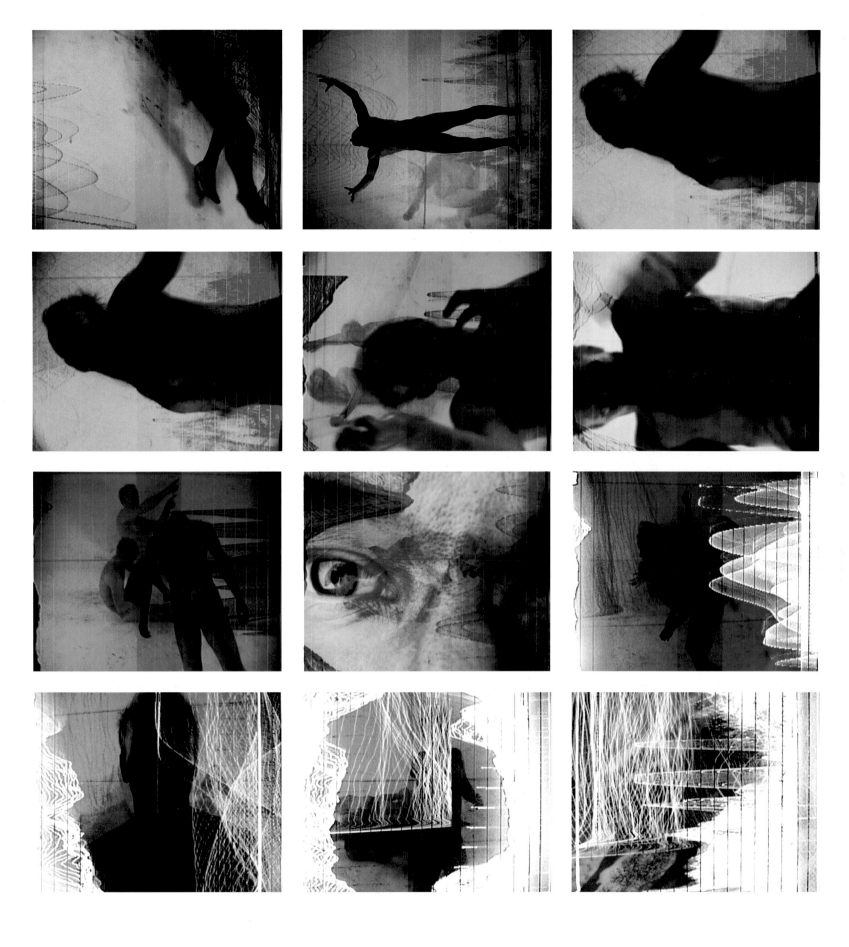

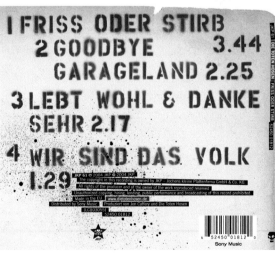

Design Dirk Rudolph
Music Die Toten Hosen
Format CD Covers

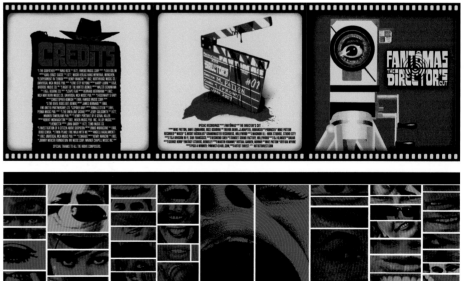

Design   Martin Kvamme
Music   Fantomas
Format   CD Cover, Tour Poster

Jim O'Rourke & Mirror *Japan Tour*

9/14 MIRROR & JIM O'ROURKE / JIM O'ROURKE SOLO at L@N Akasaka
   LIVE: Mirror & Jim O'Rourke, Jim O'Rourke (solo live)
9/15 MIRROR & JIM O'ROURKE -presented by SPUTNIK- at Roppongi Hills Information Center / THINK ZONE
   LIVE: Mirror & Jim O'Rourke, Kozo Inada & Philip Samartzis, Toshimaru Nakamura
9/16 JIM O'ROURKE & FRIENDS at Aoyama CAY
   LIVE: Jim O'Rourke (solo live & DJ), Sangatsu, Otomo Yoshihide (guiter solo) / DJ: Akira Sasaki (HEADZ)
9/17 JIM O'ROURKE & MIRROR IN KYOTO -still echo- at Kyoto CLUB METRO
   LIVE: Jim O'Rourke (solo live), Mirror & Jim O'Rourke, Assembler (Nobukazu Takemura) / DJ: Kazuma

Total Information: HEADZ (03-3770-5721) http://www.faderbyheadz.com

Design	Akira Sasaki	Mike King
Music	Jim O'Rourke & Mirror	Sleater Kinney
Format	Flyer	Gig Poster

MUSIC FOR ADULTS
LIVE! IN THE 7TH STREET ENTRY

MAY 17TH 2003

the MAGNOLIAS

Tickets priced at eight dollars, Doors open at 8:00pm

UNCENSORED

design by KINGMINI.com

PLAIN PARADE PRESENTS:

THE TROUBLE WITH SWEENEY

RECORD RELEASE PARTY

with special guests
ELK CITY, AMERICAN ALTITUDE and CRUEL SUMMER DJS

Charity Cathy, Sara Sherr and Trishylicious
FRIDAY APRIL 11 • 9PM at UACA HALL

847 North Franklin Street (near Poplar)

For more info: www.thetroublewithsweeney.com, www.buranttoastvinyl.com, www.plainparade.org
The Trouble With Sweeney - I Know You Destroy Out nationwide on Burnt Toast Vinyl on April 22.
Stay tuned for more info on contests, instores and more.

SCENE CREAMERS
Featuring Ian & Michelle from Make Up
Thursday, March 27th
In the 7th St. Entry

AN EVENING WITH
WEEN
ROCKEFELLER
FRE. 28 NOVEMBER

FORSALG BILLETTSERVICE POSTEN 815 33 133
DØRENE ÅPNER 2000 OBS TIDLIG KONSERT START!
18 ÅRS ALDERSGRENSE LEG. PLIKT
NYTT ALBUM «QUEBEC» FÅES KJØPT DER CDS SELGES

YO LA TENGO

WITH THE AISLERS SET
HIGHER GROUND

PHIL A.SHEO WITH THE GOODS
AUGUST 16TH / THE CONTINENTAL + TWO MAN ADVANTAGE

Design	KMI	Heads of State	Martin Kvamme	JDK	Studio 1800
Music	The Magnolias, Scene Creamers	The Trouble with Sweeney	Ween	Yo La Tengo	...with the Goods
Format	Gig Posters	Gig Poster	Gig Poster	Gig Poster	Gig Poster

Design   Dirk Bonsma
Music   Various
Format   Gig Posters

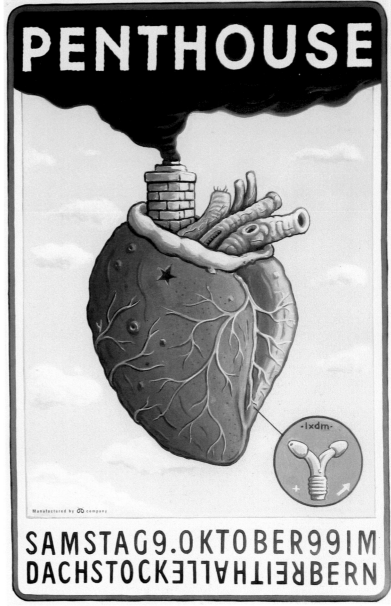

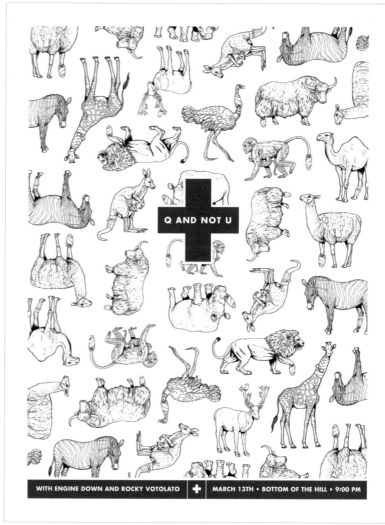

Design	Small Stakes	Heads of State	Mike King	F27
Music	Alkaline Trio, Q not an U	Karate	Interpol	Spoon
Format	Gig Posters	Gig Poster	Gig Poster	Gig Poster

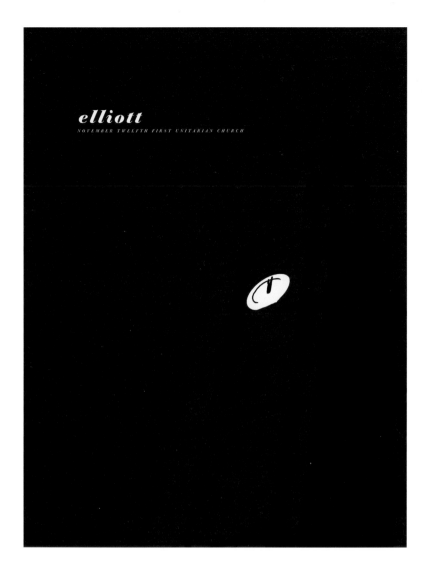

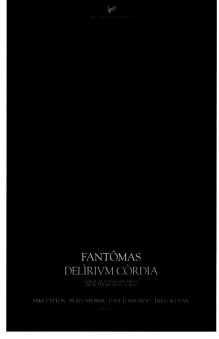

Design	Heads of State	F27	Martin Kvamme
Music	Elliott, Sputnik, Owls	Doves	Fantomas
Format	Gig Posters	Gig Poster	Gig Poster

GOLDENVOICE.COM PRESENTS
THURSDAY OCTOBER 31ST · $17.50
DASHBOARD CONFESSIONAL
HOT ROD CIRCUIT · RHETT MILLER · PIEBALD
THE PALLADIUM · 6215 SUNSET BLVD · HOLLYWOOD, CA

WWW.BRIANEWING.COM

297

Design	Emek	2Yang
Music	Various	Aba Shanti-I
Format	Gig Posters	Gig Poster

THE WHITE STRIPES

HAMBURG, GERMANY

DIENSTAG, 20. MAI   GROSSE FREIHEIT   PRÄSENTIERT VON KARSTEN JAHNKE

Design	Justin Hampton
Music	White Stripes
Format	Gig Poster

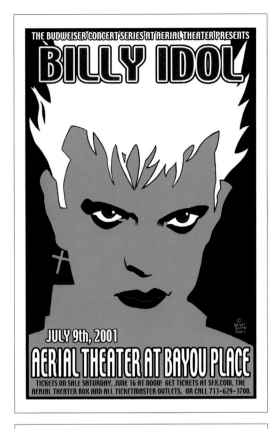

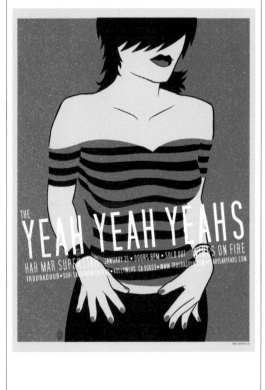

Design   Brian Ewing
Music   Various
Format   Gig Posters

304

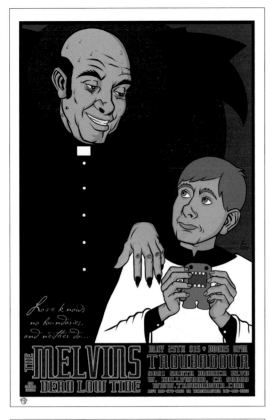

Design   Emek
Music   White Stripes + Yeah Yeah Yeah's
Format   Gig Poster

Design Heads of State 33rpm Tsuyoshi Hirooka Methane 33rpm Asterik
Music Modest Mouse Le Tigre Wanna Rock The Fags Mirah Papa Roach
Format Gig Poster Gig Poster Gig Poster Gig Poster Gig Poster Gig Poster

307

MAGNET
JIM STÄRK

ROCKEFELLER **TORSDAG 15 JANUAR 2004** BILL KR 160

Design   Rune Mortensen   Dyhr.Hagen   Victoria Collier
Music   Jim Stärk, Magnet Swan Lee   Neil Halstead
Format   Poster   CD Cover   CD Cover

Beth Orton

WITH GUESTS HEM AND ALEX LLOYD
HIGHER GROUND, WINOOSKI, VERMONT
08.02.02

Design   Burnfield
Music   Pluxus
Format   CD Cover

Design   Gink
Music   The Vines
Format   Gig Poster

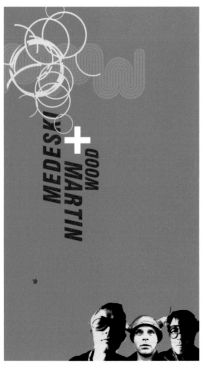

Design	Studio 1800	Shrine	Martin Kvamme	Mike King
Music	The Boggs	Medeski	Lamb	Flatstock
Format	Tour Posters	Poster	Gig Poster	Poster

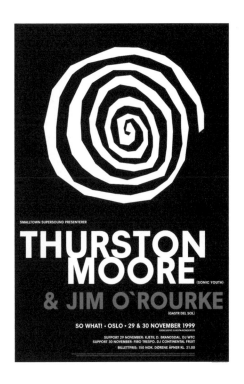

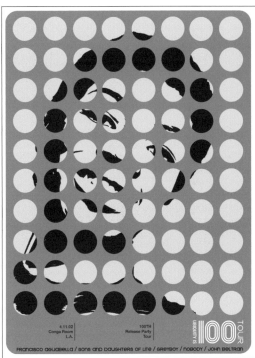

Design   Rune Mortensen   Hydrafuse   National Forest

Music   Lambchop, Yo La Tengo, Thurton Moore   Weezer   Ubiquity

Format   Gig Posters   Tour Poster   Tour Poster

PEDRO THE LiON

catacombs NOV.16 8:30PM $10

POSTER: 33RPM

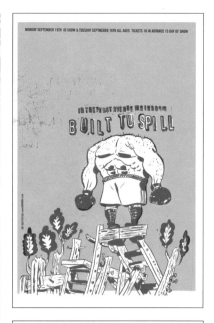

MONDAY SEPTEMBER 15TH ID SHOW & TUESDAY SEPTEMBER 16TH ALL AGES TICKETS 10 IN ADVANCE 15 DAY OF SHOW

IN THE FIRST AVENUE MAINROOM
BUILT TO SPILL

JOHNNY MARR + THE HEALERS
Wednesday, May 7th in the FIRST AVENUE MAINROOM

TICKETS 20 IN ADVANCE OR 20.00 AT THE DOOR | DOORS OPEN AT 6:00PM | ID SHOW

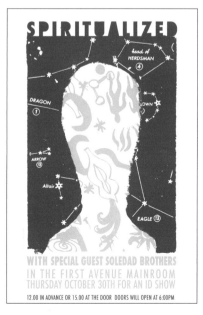

SPIRITUALIZED

head of
HERDSMAN 4

DRAGON 7

OWN

ARROW 13

Altair

EAGLE 13

WITH SPECIAL GUEST SOLEDAD BROTHERS
IN THE FIRST AVENUE MAINROOM
THURSDAY OCTOBER 30TH FOR AN ID SHOW

12.00 IN ADVANCE OR 15.00 AT THE DOOR DOORS WILL OPEN AT 6:00PM

Design	33rpm	KMI
Music	Pedro, the Lion	Built to Spill, Johnny Marr, Spiritualized
Format	Gig Poster	Gig Poster

Design   33rpm   KMI
Music   The Turn-Ons   Pedro, the Lion, The Lonesome Organist, Thermals
Format   Gig Poster   Gig Posters

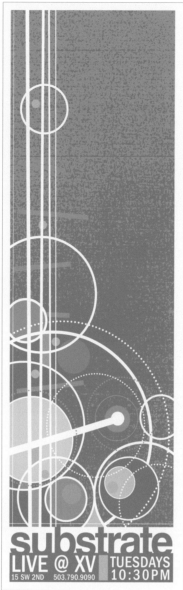

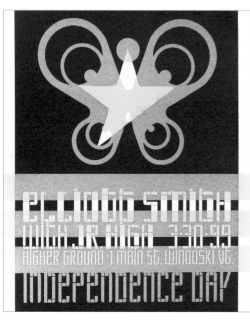

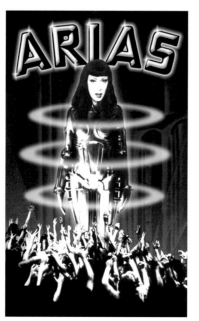

Design	33rpm	JDK	Mike King
Music	FCS North	Elliot Smith	Substrate, Wire, Arias
Format	Gig Poster	Gig Poster	Gig Poster

BEN KWELLER AND DEATH CAB FOR CUTIE
SPRING TOUR 2004

DEATH CAB FOR CUTIE AND BEN KWELLER
SPRING TOUR 2004

THEAMERICANANALOGSET

LES SAVY FAV
GREAT AMERICAN MUSIC HALL
NOVEMBER 26 | 8PM

AGAINST ME!
MAY 10 | WITH FIFTH HOUR HERO | 924 GILMAN STREET, BERKELEY

PEDRO THE LION GREAT AMERICAN MUSIC HALL
W/ SELDOM + SCIENTIFIC **NOVEMBER 25 $12 8PM**

U.S. TOUR 2003

SUGARCULT

WITH STORY OF THE YEAR, JACKSON AND PLAIN WHITE T'S

WHY? WITH CRIME IN CHOIR AND THE MOORE BROTHERS W/ NEDELLE AT THE RAMP ON AUGUST 17TH AT 7PM FOR 6 DOLLARS

FALL TOUR **DEATH CAB FOR CUTIE** W/ NADA SURF

2003

04

FLATSTOCK

SPONSORED BY SXSW & THE AMERICAN POSTER INSTITUTE
AUSTIN CONVENTION CENTER | MARCH 19 – 20, 2004

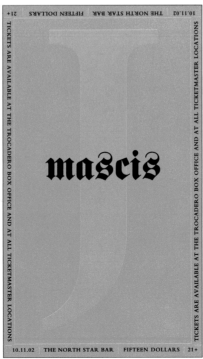

Design   Heads of State
Music   Various
Format   Gig Posters

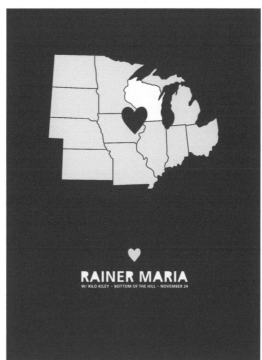

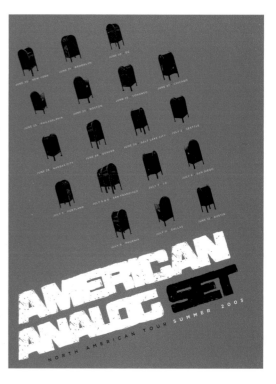

Design	Heads of State	Small Stakes	Mike King
Music	Cat Power, American Analog Set	Rainer Maria, The Decemberists	The Klezmatics
Format	Gig Posters	Gig Posters	Gig Poster

Friday, July 26th

DESAPARECIDOS

First Unitarian Church

THE DILLINGER ESCAPE PLAN

WITH SPECIAL GUESTS DALEK
FRIDAY DECEMBER 21 7PM
FIRST UNITARIAN CHURCH 22ND & CHESTNUT
ADMISSION $8 WWW.R5PRODUCTIONS.COM
TICKETS AVAILABLE AT SPACEBOY RECORDS

MANUFACTURED BY
CAPTAINS OF INDUSTRY
PHILADELPHIA, PA

CURSIVE

EASTERN YOUTH · FIN FANG FOOM
WEDNESDAY SEPTEMBER 24 · ALLEY KATZ · 8PM · $10.00
FREE TO VCU + UR STUDENTS

HOT HOT HEAT

JUNE 30 · FIRST UNITARIAN CHURCH
WITH THE MOVING UNITS · ALL AGES

ROB CROW

W/ HELLA + CASTANETS — FEBRUARY 22 — THE RAMP — 2236 PARKER, BERKELEY — 7PM

Design   Small Stakes
Music   Rob Grow
Format   Gig Poster

324

PRE†TY
GIRLS
MAKE
GRAVES

SMALL BROWN BIKE
BREAKING PANGEA
THURSDAY MARCH SEVENTH
FIRST UNITARIAN CHURCH

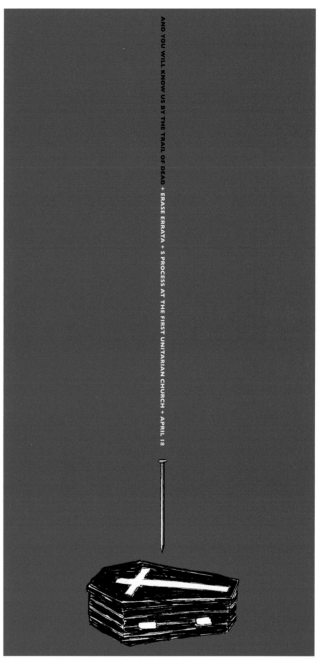

AND YOU WILL KNOW US BY THE TRAIL OF DEAD + ERASE ERRATA + S PROCESS AT THE FIRST UNITARIAN CHURCH + APRIL 18

Design   Heads of State
Music   Various
Format   Gig Posters

the Rapture

FALL TOUR 2003

Oberlin • Detroit • Chicago • Minneapolis • Seattle • Portland • San Francisco • Los Angeles • San Diego • Tuscon • Denver
Omaha • Lawrence • St Louis • Columbus • Newport • Washington • Boston • Providence • Philadelphia • New York

Design   Studio 1800
Music   The Rapture
Format   Gig Poster

BUILT TO SPILL

OCTOBER SECOND · THE TROCADERO · PHILADELPHIA

WITH SOLACE BROTHERS & THE DELUSIONS

Design	Heads of State
Music	Built To Spill
Format	Gig Poster

62/ DESIGN: MAIK BLUHM / 18.OKTOBER • MUSIC: NORTHERN LITE, MONOSURROUND, GUNJAH • VINYL SLEEVES: NORTHERN LITE: "GONE", "GONE / REACH THE SUN – PROMO", "REACH THE SUN", WWW.NORTHERNLITE.DE, • MONOSURROUND VS. RACCOON BROTHERS: "CREEPY GUYS", WWW.MONOSURROUND.DE • GUNJAH: "FUNKWELT" • LABEL: 1ST DECADE RECORDS, WWW.1STDECADE.DE, VIDEOSTILL: ERIK NIEDLING, WWW.FOTORAUM.DE (FOR ALL)

64/ DESIGN: FACTOR PRODUKT • MUSIC: CONNECTED COMPILATION • CD PACKAGE

66 DESIGN: A.LORENZ • MUSIC: AGF • VINYL SLEEVE, CD COVER, "HEAD SLASH BAUCH", 2001.09, CD DIGIPAK AND LP SLEEVE, ORTHLORNG MUSORK, SAN FRANCISCO 2002, ORTH08
DESIGN: MFRESH • MUSIC: FONTANELLE • CD COVER

67 DESIGN: A.LORENZ • MUSIC: ELECTRIC COMPANY • CD COVER, "GREATEST HITS", 2001.07CD SLEEVE, PHOTO: ASSOCIATED PRESS/STEVE MILLER, JANUARY 2001, TIGERBEAT6, OAKLAND 2001, MEOW032
DESIGN: HYDRAFUSE • MUSIC: ROBERT NANNA/ELISABETH ELMORE • VINYL SLEEVE

68 DESIGN: IO • MUSIC: SVENSON • CD COVER, "SEE YOU IN EARTH", 2002, LABEL: CAR CRASH.

69 DESIGN: NITRADA • MUSIC: NITRADA • CD COVER
DESIGN: DAVID SCHELLNEGGER • MUSIC: JULLANDER • CD COVER

70 DESIGN: FACTOR PRODUKT • MUSIC: SLUT • CD COVER, BOOK

71 DESIGN: FACTOR PRODUKT • MUSIC: MILLENIA NOVA • CD COVER, BOOK

72 DESIGN: FACTOR PRODUKT • MUSIC: THOM • CD COVER, BOOK

73 DESIGN: DIRK RUDOLPH • MUSIC: REAMONN • CD COVER
DESIGN: FACTOR PRODUKT • MUSIC: EMIL BULLS • CD COVERS, BOOK

74 DESIGN: A.LORENZ, ALEXANDER OBST • MUSIC: MAXIMILIAN HECKER • CD COVERS, DESIGN-KONZEPT/PHOTOGRAPHY: ALEXANDER OBST, WWW.ALEXANDEROBST.DE, LABEL: KITTY-YO, WWW.KITTY-YO.COM

75 DESIGN: BIG ACTIVE • MUSIC: NIO • CD COVER, "SPECIAL" SINGLE, THE ECHO LABEL, 2003, ART DIRECTION & DESIGN: MAT MAITLAND, RICHARD ANDREWS @ BIG ACTIVE, PHOTOS: KLAUS THYMANN
DESIGN: MIKE KING • MUSIC: JACK JOHNSON • CD COVER, PHOTOS: JP PLUNIER
DESIGN: SURFACE • MUSIC: AUCH • CD COVERS, "KISS TOMORROW GOODBYE", "REMIX TOMORROW GOODBYE", LABEL: MILLE PLATEAUX
DESIGN: AKIRA SASAKI • MUSIC: BATOFAR • FLYER

76 DESIGN: KIM HIORTHØY • MUSIC: KIM HIORTHØY • VINYL SLEEVE, HOPENESS E.P.12", LABEL: SMALLTOWN SUPERSOUND, 2004
DESIGN: ASTERIK • MUSIC: NORMA • CD COVER
DESIGN: FAT CAT • MUSIC: HIM • VINYL SLEEVE
DESIGN: EH? > EHQUESTIONMARK • MUSIC: DJ SIGNIFY • VINYL INNER SLEEVE, LEX RECORDS 024, WWW.LEXRECORDS.COM

77 DESIGN: JONAS GROSSMANN > ENV @ SOURCE • MUSIC: ADRIEN 75 • CD COVER, "COASTAL ACCESS", LABEL: SOURCE, 2002, WWW.SOURCE-RECORDS. COM
DESIGN: A.LORENZ • MUSIC: DONNACHA COSTELLO • VINYL SLEEVE, CD COVER, "GROWING UP IN PUBLIC", 2000.08, CD JEWEL-BOX AND DLP SLEEVE, FORCE INC., FRANKFURT/MAIN 2000, FIM198 (DLP), FIM-1-043 (CD)
DESIGN: STYLOROUGE • MUSIC: MIKE LINDUP • CD COVER
DESIGN: MFRESH • MUSIC: CHARLES ATLAS • CD COVER

78 DESIGN: MAIK BLUHM / 18.OKTOBER • MUSIC: NORTHERN LITE • CD COVERS, NORTHERN LITE: "TREAT ME BETTER", "MY PAIN", WWW.NORTHERNLITE.DE, • (FOR ALL:) LABEL: 1ST DECADE RECORDS, WWW.1STDECADE.DE, VIDEOSTILL: ERIK NIEDLING, WWW.FOTORAUM.DE

79 DESIGN: UNIVERSAL EVERYTHING • MUSIC: TUJIKO NORIKO • CD COVER, "FROM TOKYO TO NAIAGARA", LABEL: TOMLAB, 2003
DESIGN: NONFORMAT • MUSIC: CURSOR MINER • VINYL SLEEVE, CD COVER, "EXPLOSIVE PIECE OF MIND", PHOTOGRAPHY BY JAKE WALTERS, 2002
DESIGN: K7! • MUSIC: SHANTEL • VINYL SLEEVE
DESIGN: PFADFINDEREI • MUSIC: ELLEN ALIEN • VINYL SLEEVE

80 DESIGN: ZION • MUSIC: ECLECTIC BOB • CD COVER
DESIGN: FONS HICKMANN, SABINE WILMS • MUSIC: NONEX • CD COVER, "LADYFITNESS", CLIENT: NONEX, STUDIO: FONS HICKMANN M23

81 DESIGN: KARLSSONWILKER • MUSIC: EFTIR BÖGN • CD COVER, BOOK

82/ DESIGN: MINUS • MUSIC: EINSTÜRZENDE NEUBAUTEN • CD COVERS, „PERPETUUM MOBILE", PHOTO: ANNO DITTMER, „STRATEGIES AGAINST ARCHITECTURES III", PHOTO: ANNO DITTMER, „9-15-2000, BRUSSELS", „PERPETUUM MOBILE TOUR 2004"

84 DESIGN: ZION • MUSIC: USER • CD COVER
DESIGN: STYLOROUGE • MUSIC: THE ORDINARY BOYS • CD COVER

85 DESIGN: TINA FRANK • MUSIC: JIM O'ROURKE • CD COVER, "I'M HAPPY, AND I'MSINGING, AND A 1,2,3,4", LABEL: MEGO, 2002
DESIGN: APT. 13 • MUSIC: THE HAL AL SHEDAD • "DICHOTOMY OF YESTERDAY", 7 INCH SINGLE, SIMBA RECORDS
DESIGN: RED • MUSIC: RED SNAPPER • CD COVER, „SOME KIND OF KINK"
DESIGN: RUNE MORTENSEN • MUSIC: MUO - MUSIC UNDER OSLO • CD COVER, LABEL: DBUT RECORDS, 2002

86 DESIGN: RUNE MORTENSEN • MUSIC: JAZZ CD COMPILATION • CD PACKAGE, "JAZZCD.NO", LABEL: NORSK JAZZFORUM, 2003

87 DESIGN: RUNE MORTENSEN • MUSIC: J.R.EWING • CD COVER, "LAUGHING WITH DAGGERS", LABEL: PRIMITIVE RECORDS, 2002

88 DESIGN: ROBERT SAMSONOWITZ • MUSIC: PLEJ • CD/VINYL COVER, "ELECTRONIC MUSIC FROM THE SWEDISH LEFTCOAST", LABEL: : EXCEPTIONAL RECORDS, 2003, PLEJ LOGOTYPE BY ARVID NIKLASSON.

89 DESIGN: SPEZIALMATERIAL • MUSIC: SPEZIALMATERIAL COMPILATION • VARIOUS ARTISTS: «3», 2003, GRAFIK: TOBIAS PEIER, WWW.BODARA.CH, PHOTO: TERESA SALERNO, SALERNO.TERESA@GMX.CH

90 DESIGN: HIDEKI INABA • MUSIC: E2-E4 • VINYL SLEEVE, COMPILATION FEAT. DUB SQUAD, ROVO, SUGAR PLANT, KAI, HI SPEED AND STARLIGHT EXPRESS, SMURF OTOKOGUMI, BUFFALO DAUGHTER, 2001, CLIENT: ELECTRIC SAL/DAIICHI KOSHO CO.,LTD.

91 DESIGN: SUPERLOW • MUSIC: EARTH 2 • VINYL SLEEVE
DESIGN: JDK • MUSIC: INTERPOL • GIG POSTER, STUDIO – JAGER DI PAOLA KEMP DESIGN, BURLINGTON, VT.; CREATIVE DIRECTOR – MICHAEL JAGER; DESIGN DIRECTOR – MALCOLM BUICK; DESIGN – JOHN SIDDLE; PRINTING – ISKRA SCREENPRINTING COOP
DESIGN: JONAS GROSSMANN > ENV @ SOURCE • MUSIC: OPEN SOURCE • CD COVER, "OPENSOURCE.CODE", LABEL: SOURCE, 2002, WWW.SOURCE-RECORDS. COM
DESIGN: ICON • MUSIC: JÜRGEN DE BLONDE • CD COVER, "HIDDEN RABBIT", LABEL: TOMLAB

92/ DESIGN: DIRK RUDOLPH • MUSIC: SONO • CD COVERS, BOOKS, "2000 GUNS", "BLAME"

94 DESIGN: WUFF • MUSIC: IAN POOLEY • VINYL SLEEVE, LABELCOVER FOR POOLEDMUSIC.
DESIGN: PFADFINDEREI • MUSIC: SASCHA FUNKE • VINYL SLEEVE
DESIGN: BURNFIELD • MUSIC: PLUXEMBURG • FLYER, 2003 (WWW.PLUXEMBURG.COM)

95 DESIGN: THRILL JOCKEY • MUSIC: SUE GARNER • CD COVER
DESIGN: THRILL JOCKEY • MUSIC: OVAL • CD COVER
DESIGN: HYDRAFUSE • MUSIC: MATES OF STATE • CD COVER, POSTE

96 DESIGN: BIG ACTIVE • MUSIC: SPAN • CD COVERS, "MASS DISTRACTION" ALBUM, "FOUND" SINGLE, "PAPA" SINGLE, "DON'T THINK" SINGLE, ALL UNIVERSAL/ISLAND, 2003/2004, ART DIRECTION: RICHARD ANDREWS, GERARD SAINT @ BIG ACTIVE, DESIGN: RICHARD ANDREWS @ BIG ACTIVE, ILLUSTRATIONS: DAVID FOLDVARI @ BIG ACTIVE

97 DESIGN: BIG ACTIVE • MUSIC: I AM KLOOT • CD COVERS, "3 FEET TALL" 2 SINGLES, THE ECHO LABEL, 2003, ART DIRECTION & DESIGN: MAT MAITLAND @ BIG ACTIVE, ILLUSTRATION: KATE GIBB @ BIG ACTIVE
DESIGN: BIG ACTIVE • MUSIC: SIMIAN • CD COVERS, "FRIENDS" ALBUM, "NEVER BE ALONE" SINGLE, "LA BREEZE" SINGLE, "ONE DIMENSION" SINGLE, ALL SOURCE RECORDS U.K./VIRGIN, 2003, ART DIRECTION & DESIGN: MAT MAITLAND @ BIG ACTIVE, ILLUSTRATION: KATE GIBB @ BIG ACTIVE

98 DESIGN: MOSS DESIGN UNIT • MUSIC: COSMIC VILLAGE • CD COVERS, VINYL SLEEVES "T.B.D.", AD+D: SACHI SAWADA, LABEL: FORLIFE RECORDS, 2001
DESIGN: BÜRO DESTRUCT • MUSIC: GIVE PEAS A CHANCE • COMPILATION LP- AND CD-SLEEVE, DESIGNER: LOPETZ, CLIENT: CRIPPLED DICK HOT WAX, BERLIN, 2002
DESIGN: BÜRO DESTRUCT • MUSIC: LUKE VIBERT • FLYER AND POSTER, DESIGNER: LOPETZ, CLIENT: REITSCHULE BERN, 2003
DESIGN: BÜRO DESTRUCT • MUSIC: NINJATUNE • FLYER AND POSTER, DESIGNER: LOPETZ, CLIENT: REITSCHULE BERN, 2001
DESIGN: NONFORMAT • MUSIC: LUKE VIBERT • VINYL SLEEVE, "FURTHER NUGGETS" COMPILATION.
DESIGN: STRUGGLE • MUSIC: MOS DEF • VINYL SLEEVE, "MOS DEF & DIVERSE", LABEL: CHOCOLATE INDUSTRIES
DESIGN: DIRK RUDOLPH • MUSIC: LAMBRETTA • CD COVER
DESIGN: RUNE MORTENSEN • MUSIC: PAAL NILSSEN-LOVE / MADS GUSTAFSSON • CD COVER, "I LOVE IT WHEN YOU SNORE", LABEL: SMALLTOWN SUPERSOUND, 2002
DESIGN: IO • MUSIC: CAESARS PALACE • SINGLE COVER, "JERK IT OUT", LABEL: DOLORES RECORDINGS/VIRGIN RECORDS, 2002.
DESIGN: SO TAKAHASHI • MUSIC: NUBUS • CD COVER

99 DESIGN: KIM HIORTHØY • MUSIC: JAGA JAZZIST, DAVID GRUBBS • CD COVERS, VINYL SLEEVES: JAGA JAZZIST: THE STIX, LABEL: SMALLTOWN SUPERSOUND/NINJA TUNE, 2003 • DAVID GRUBBS: A GUESS AT THE RIDDLE, LABEL: DRAG CITY/FAT CAT, 2004

100 DESIGN: SLANG INTERNATIONAL • MUSIC: KID 606 • VINYL SLEEVE, "KILL SOUND BEFORE SOUND KILLS YOU", 12" RECORD COVER, CLIENT: TIGERBEAT6 / IPECAC RECORDINGS, LOCATION: OAKLAND, 2003
DESIGN: SLANG INTERNATIONAL • MUSIC: GOLD CHAINS • VINYL SLEEVE, 12" RECORD COVER, CLIENT: ORTHLORNG MUSORK, LOCATION: SAN FRANCISCO, 2001

101 DESIGN: NATIONAL FOREST • MUSIC: LÉ SOUND IN COLOR SERIES • 7" SLEEVES

102/ DESIGN: SPEZIALMATERIAL • MUSIC: VARIOUS • CD COVER: SOLOTEMPO: "OCD:TEN", SM007LP001 & SM007CD005, 2002, GRAPHICS: TOBIAS.PEIER, WWW.BODARA.CH, INDUSTRIAL DESIGN: CHIARA NIKISCH, WWW.POE-TITI.CH • FLYER: VARIOUS, GRAPHICS: TOBIAS PEIER, WWW.BODARA.CH

103 DESIGN: AKIRA SASAKI • MUSIC: SCANNER + D-FUSE • FLYER

104 DESIGN: AKIRA SASAKI • MUSIC: RIOW ARAI • CD PACKAGING, VINYL SLEEVE: ALBUM COVER DESIGN FOR RIOW ARAI'S DEVICE PEOPLE
DESIGN: SPEZIALMATERIAL • MUSIC: VARIOUS • FLYER: SPEZIALMATERIAL/SHITKATAPULT, GRAPHICS: TOBIAS PEIER, WWW.BODARA.CH

105 DESIGN: JOHN WIESE • MUSIC: JOHN WIESE • GATEFOLD LP, SISSY SPACEK "SCISSORS", LABEL: MISANTHROPIC AGENDA, 2003, ILLUSTRATION: JESSE JACKSON
DESIGN: SLANG INTERNATIONAL • MUSIC: APPARAT • VINYL SLEEVE, "TTTRIAL AND EROR", 12" RECORD COVER, CLIENT: SHITKATAPULT, LOCATION: BERLIN, 2001
DESIGN: NICOLAS BOURQUIN • MUSIC: STEINBRÜCHEL • VINYL SLEEVES

106 DESIGN: SPEZIALMATERIAL • MUSIC: "FROM PERSON TO YOU", SM003EP001 & SM003CDROM001, 2002, GRAPHICS: TOBIAS.PEIER, WWW.BODARA.CH, DESIGN: CHIARA NIKISCH, WWW.POE-TITI.CH

107 DESIGN: REGINA • MUSIC: NINE DAYS WONDER • VINYL SLEEVE
DESIGN: UNIVERSAL EVERYTHING • MUSIC: LAB 01 • LP GATEFOLD / CD DIGIPAK, "ADVANCED PUBLIC LISTENING 1", LABEL: LABORATORY INSTINCT
DESIGN: RALPH STEINBRÜCHEL • MUSIC: STEINBRÜCHEL/ BRUSA • CD PACKAGING, "RED8.4-" MINI CD-R, LABEL: SYNCHRON > SYNC02, WWW.SYNCHRON.CH, MINI CD-R IN BLACK ENVELOPE, BLACK/SILVER, PHOTO CREDIT: PETER WÜRMLI

108 DESIGN: SPEZIALMATERIAL • MUSIC: VARIOUS • VINYL SLEEVES 01, 03, 05, 08

109 DESIGN: RALPH STEINBRÜCHEL • MUSIC: VARIOUS • VINYL SLEEVES, "GRANULAT_LIVE_SERIES" 4X 7" VINYL SINGLE, LABEL: SYNCHRON > SYNC01, , WWW.SYNCHRON.CH, 7" SINGLES IN ENVELOPE, 1-COLOR-PRINT: BLACK, VISUALS INSERT: TESTEAM, LABEL PHOTO CREDIT: PETER WÜRMLISINGLE 1 : SEITE A : ERROR1 : SEITE B : VERSION2 : SINGLE 2 : SEITE A : SOLAR3 : SEITE B : FLOPPY4 : SINGLE 3 : SEITE A : END5 : SEITE B : SIXSIX6 : SINGLE 4 : SEITE A : 00SIEBEN : SEITE B : CONTACT8 : CARDS FOR "RED8.4-" MINI CD-R, LABEL: SYNCHRON > SYNC02, WWW.SYNCHRON.CH

110 DESIGN: A. LORENZ • MUSIC: VARIOUS • VINYL SLEEVES, RITORNELL SERIES1999.08–2000.11, CD SERIES, 6PP CARDBOARD SLEEVES, CUSTOM FORMAT | 1 SPOT COLOUR EACH + BLACK, (FOR THE BARCODE), RITORNELL, FRANKFURT/MAIN, 1999–2000 | RIT04–RIT19 • V/A: GOOD NIGHT – MUSIC TO SLEEP BY, 2003.03, DCD SLEEVE, JEWELBOX, TIGERBEAT6, OAKLAND 2003 | MEOW006
DESIGN: THRILL JOCKEY • MUSIC: THE SEA AND CAKE • CD COVER
DESIGN: MFRESH • MUSIC: KID 606 • GIG POSTER

111 DESIGN: A. LORENZ • MUSIC: VARIOUS • VINYL SLEEVES, CD COVERS: ATMO.BRTSCHITSCH: ROCKSTAR EP, 2003.10, 12" SLEEVE | 4C CMYK, SILKE MAURER, BERLIN 2004 | SIM02 • WHITE HOLE: HOLY GHOST EP, 2003.10, 12" SLEEVE | 4C CMYK, SILKE MAURER, BERLIN 2004 | SIM03 • ATMO.BRTSCHITSCH: CHANGE YOUR LIFE, 2003.08, CD SLEEVE, DIGIPAK | 4C CMYK, SILKE MAURER, BERLIN 2003 | SIM01 • FULL SWING: [EDITS] CD, 2001.09, CD SLEEVE, 4PP DIGIPAK | 1C PANTONE, ORTHLORNG MUSORK, SAN FRANCISCO 2002 | ORTH05.CD

112 DESIGN: D-REALM • MUSIC: VARIOUS • VINYL SLEEVES

113 DESIGN: SURFACE • MUSIC: COCOON COMPILATIONS • VINYL SLEEVES, LABEL: COCOON
DESIGN: ZION • MUSIC: OUTFUNK • VINYL SLEEVE

114 DESIGN: A.LORENZ • MUSIC: VARIOUS • VINYL SLEEVES, CD COVERS, STEPHAN MATHIEU, EKKEHARD EHLERS: HEROIN, 2001.03, CD SLEEVE, CUSTOM PAPER FOLDED SLEEVE | 2 SPOT COLOURS, STENCIL PRINT, COLLABORATIVE WORK WITH STEPHAN MATHIEU, PACKAGING CONCEPT / PRINT: EXTRAPOOL, NIJMEGEN, THE NETHERLANDS STAALPLAAT/EXTRAPOOL, AMSTERDAM/ NIJMEGEN 2001 | BROMBRON02 • FULL SWING EP2000.02,12" SLEEVE, ORTHLORNG MUSORK, SAN FRANCISCO 2000 | ORTH03 • FULL SWING [EDITS] SERIES, 2000.10–2001.09, FIVE 10" SLEEVES | 1 SPOT COLOUR EACH, ORTHLORNG MUSORK, SAN FRANCISCO 2000–2001 | ORTH05.1–ORTH05.5

115 DESIGN: A.LORENZ • MUSIC: RECHENZENTRUM • CD COVERS, VINYL SLEEVES, POSTERS, "DIRECTOR'S CUT", 2003.03, CD/DVD DIGIPAK AND DLP SLEEVE, ILLUSTRATION: VIDEO STILLS, TAKEN FROM THE DVDMILLE PLATEAUX, FRANKFURT/MAIN 2001 | MP120 • THE JOHN PEEL SESSION, 2001.05, CD DIGIPAK AND DLP SLEE- VE, ILLUSTRATION: PAPER CUT, UNKNOWN AUTHOR, HONG KONG, KITTY-YO INT., BERLIN 2001, KY01047CD/LP • "RECHENZENTRUM", 2000.04, CD DIGIPAK AND DLP SLEEVE, KITTY-YO INT., BERLIN 2000 KY00030CD/DLP

116 DESIGN: PFADFINDEREI • MUSIC: VARIOUS • VINYL SLEEVES
DESIGN: RUNE MORTENSEN • MUSIC: RÖYKSOPP & VARIOUS ARTISTS • POSTER, 2001

117 DESIGN: AKIRA SASAKI • MUSIC: MILLE PLATEAUX/FORCE INC. • FLYER, T-SHIRT, IMAGES

118 DESIGN: MONITOR POP • MUSIC: APPLETON & TREU • CD COVER • MUSIC: EARTHLINGS • CD COVER

119 DESIGN: BOWLING CLUB • MUSIC: IT SACHS! • CD COVER

120 DESIGN: KARLSSONWILKER • MUSIC: HATTLER • CD COVERS, POSTERS

121 DESIGN: KARLSSONWILKER • MUSIC: ELEMENTAL CHILL SERIES • CD COVERS

122 DESIGN: KARLSSONWILKER • MUSIC: KRAAN • CD COVER, POSTER
DESIGN: DISCODOENER • MUSIC: MOTION UNIT • CD COVER

123 DESIGN: AIRSIDE • MUSIC: WAX POETIC • VINYL SLEEVE, "ANGELS"

124 DESIGN: F27 - FACTOR 27 • MUSIC: DJ VADIM • GIG POSTER

125 DESIGN: MFRESH • MUSIC: NUDGE • GIG POSTER

126 DESIGN: STRUGGLE • MUSIC: PEOPLE OF RHYTHM • VINYL SLEEVE, MACHINE GENERIC SLEEVE, LABEL: POR / MACHINE RECORDS
DESIGN: RED • MUSIC: TERRY CALLIER • CD COVER

127 DESIGN: DAG • MUSIC: VARIOUS • CD COVERS, VINYL SLEEVES

128 DESIGN: CARLOS SEGURA • MUSIC: LESLEY SPENCER • CD COVER, POSTER, FLYER (ANTHEM)

129 DESIGN: TORTOISE • MUSIC: TORTOISE • CD COVER
DESIGN: FAT CAT • MUSIC: XINLI SUPREME • CD COVER

130 DESIGN: TSUYOSHI KUSANO • MUSIC: COLLIDER • VARIOUS • MUSIC: EXTERMINATE • VARIOUS
DESIGN: BIG ACTIVE • MUSIC: KINESIS • CD COVERS, "BILLBOARD BEAUTY" SINGLE, "AND THEY OBEY" SINGLE, ALL INDEPENDIENTE, 2003, ART DIRECTION & DESIGN: MAT MAITLAND @ BIG ACTIVE, PHOTOS: ZED NELSON

131 DESIGN: ICON • MUSIC: MOUSE ON MARS, THE BOOKS, SONIG COMPILATION • CD COVERS, THE BOOKS "THE LEMON OF PINK"", LABEL: TOMLAB • SONIG.COMP, LABEL: SONIG • MOUSE ON MARS "IDEOLOGY", LABEL: SONIG • MOUSE ON MARS "AGIT ITTER IT IT", LABEL: SONIG

132 DESIGN: JONAS GROSSMANN > ENV @ SOURCE • MUSIC: LOWTEC • CD COVER, "SECRET CORNER", LABEL: SOURCE, 2002, WWW.SOURCE-RECORDS. COM
DESIGN: JONAS GROSSMANN > ENV @ SOURCE • MUSIC: JOHAN SKUGGE • CD COVER, "OBJECTS & BUILDINGS", LABEL: SOURCE, 2002, WWW.SOURCE-RECORDS. COM
DESIGN: AKIRA SASAKI • MUSIC: RYOJI IKEDA • DESIGN FOR RYOJI IKEDA'S SOLO PERFORMANCE
DESIGN: RALPH STEINBRÜCHEL • MUSIC: VARIOUS • CD COVER "BRACKWATER", ARTISTS: TOMAS KORBER / ERIKM / TOSHIMARU NAKAMURA / OTOMO YOSHIHIDE, LABEL: FOR4EARS > CD 1550

133 DESIGN: A.LORENZ • MUSIC: KID 606 • VINYL SLEEVES, "PS I LOVE YOU", 2000.08 CD DIGIPAK AND DLP SLEEVE, MILLE PLATEAUX, FRANKFURT/MAIN 2000 | MP93 • "PS YOU LOVE ME", 2001.04, CD SLEEVE, DIGIPAK, MILLE PLATEAUX, FRANKFURT/MAIN 2001 | MP101
DESIGN: RUNE MORTENSEN • MUSIC: MONOPOT • VINYL SLEEVE, "OPTIPESS", LABEL: SMALLTOWN SUPERSOUND, 2002

134 DESIGN: ICON • MUSIC: VARIOUS • CD COVERS, OVAL"COMMERS", LABEL: ZOMBA • OVAL"SZENARIODISK", LABEL: THRILLJOCKEY • MOUSE ON MARS "NIUN NIGGUNG", LABEL: SONIG • OVAL"PRO- CESS", LABEL: ZOMBA • SONIG.ILATION, LABEL: SONIG
DESIGN: BOOGIZM • MUSIC: FYM • CD COVER

135 DESIGN: UNIVERSAL EVERYTHING • MUSIC: FLIM • CD COVER, "HELIO", LABEL: TOMLAB, 2003
DESIGN: NORMAL • MUSIC: ART OF FIGHTING • CD COVER, "WIRES", ARTWORK BY CAMERON BIRD & OLLIE BROWNE, LABEL: NORMAL RECORDS, WWW.NORMAL-RECORDS.COM
DESIGN: NITRADA • MUSIC: GIARDINI DI MIRO • CD COVERS
DESIGN: HYDRAFUSE • MUSIC: ALOHA • CD COVER

136 DESIGN: TRANSACOUSTIC RESEARCH • MUSIC: OUTPOST • EXPERIMENT, ARTWORK BY NIKOLAUS GANSTERER, LABEL: IFTAF REC (SUB-LABEL VON TRANSACOUSTIC RESEARCH), 1999

137 DESIGN: STRUGGLE • MUSIC: URBAN RENEWAL PROGRAMM • CD COVER, "SUPPLEMENT 1.5", LABEL: CHOCOLATE INDUSTRIES, ILLUSTRATION: CODY HUDSON
DESIGN: TRANSACOUSTIC RESEARCH • MUSIC: HEARINGS • CD COVER, VARIOUS ARTISTS, LABEL: TRANSACOUSTIC RESEARCH 2003, ARTWORK: MATTHIAS MEINHARTER
DESIGN: BURNFIELD • MUSIC: ROLE MODEL • SINGLE COVER, "EN TYST MINUT E.P.", 2002, LABEL: BLEEP STREET (WWW.BLEEP-STREET.COM)

138 DESIGN: DAN ABBOTT • MUSIC: MARS VOLTA • CD BOOK ILLUS-TRATION, SINGLE SLEEVE, "DE-LOUSED IN THE COMATORIUM"
DESIGN: JOHAN AND JETHRO • MUSIC: STACS OF STAMINA • VINYL SLEEVE
DESIGN: INFOPLOP • MUSIC: WHITE HEAT • THE BASEMENT, ARTIST: DARREN PICKLES, ROSS HOLLOWAY, TITLE: THEME

139 DESIGN: HIDEKI INABA • MUSIC: NAV KATZE • CD "NEVER MIND THE DISTORTIONS"/NAV KATZE REMIX BY APHEX TWIN, AUTECHRE, BLACK DOG, SUN ELECTRIC, ULTRAMARINE, GLOBAL COMMU-NICATION, RELOAD, U-ZIQ, SEEFEEL, DISJECTA, THE GENTLE PEOPLE, 2003, CLIENT: VICTOR ENTERTAINMENT,INC.,JAPAN.
DESIGN: ZIP • MUSIC: REMOTE • CD COVER

140 DESIGN: TRANSACOUSTIC RESEARCH • MUSIC: ORGANIC SYN-TESIZER • AUTOMATE: THE VEGETABLE ORCHESTRA / DAS GEMÜSE-ORCHESTER (MUSIC DONE ON VEGETABLES), LABEL: TRANSACOU-STIC RESEARCH 2003, ARTWORK: NIKOLAUS GANSTERER
DESIGN: DISKO B • MUSIC: POUTI • CD COVER
DESIGN: ENLIGHTMENT • MUSIC: MOTIVATION • CD COVER

141 DESIGN: INGORANZ • MUSIC: DIE TÜREN • CD COVER
DESIGN: DAN ABBOTT • MUSIC: MIND KIOSK • CD COVER, VINYL SLEEVE
DESIGN: TOMOKO TSUNEDA • MUSIC: PUSHIM • CD COVER

142 DESIGN: PROPELLA • MUSIC: MEDIENGRUPPE TELEKOMMANDER • VINYL SLEEVE

143 DESIGN: SWEDEN • MUSIC: DR. KOSMOS • CD COVER, BOOK, POSTER, "REPORTAGE" + EP, LABEL: MNW / NONS RECORDS, 2002 • TOUR POSTER, LABEL: NONS RECORDS, 2000

144 DESIGN: FACTOR PRODUKT • MUSIC: ÜBERSCHALL CLUB • FLYER, POSTER

145 DESIGN: FACTOR PRODUKT • MUSIC: ÜBERSCHALL CLUB • FLYER, POSTER
DESIGN: AKIRA SASAKI • MUSIC: RAFAEL TORAL, ALEJANDRA & AERON • FLYER
DESIGN: TSUYOSHI HIROOKA • MUSIC: KITCHEN • FLYER (STREET CONE ARTWORK)

146/ DESIGN: SHRINE • MUSIC: FUEL • ILLUSTRATIONS

148 DESIGN: BIG ACTIVE • MUSIC: PLEASURE • CD COVERS, "PLEASURE" ALBUM, "DON'T LOOK THE OTHER WAY" SINGLE, "THE WISP" SINGLE, "ONE DIMENSION" SINGLE, ALL CIRCUS, 2003, ART DIRECTION, COLLAGE & DESIGN: MAT MAITLAND @ BIG ACTIVE
DESIGN: SARAH LITTASY • MUSIC: TOSCA • CD COVER, "SUZUKI", LABEL: G-STONE RECORDINGS, WWW-G-STONED.COM, PHOTO-GRAPHY MARKUS RÖSSLE, TOSCA LOGO & FONT FOXY TEAM, G-STONE LOGO: WWW.OLIVERKARTAK.COM

149 DESIGN: BIG ACTIVE • MUSIC: BASEMENT JAXX • CD COVERS, "ROOTY" ALBUM, "JUST A KISS" SINGLE, "HEAD AT" SINGLE, "GET ME OFF" SINGLE, ALL XL RECORDINGS, 2001, ART DIRECTION: MAT MAITLAND, GERARD SAINT @ BIG ACTIVE, DESIGN: MAT MAITLAND @ BIG ACTIVE, ILLUSTRATIONS: RENÉ HABERMACHER @ BIG ACTIVE

150 DESIGN: BIG ACTIVE • MUSIC: LADYTRON • CD COVERS, "LIGHT & MAGIC" ALBUM, "BLUE JEANS" SINGLE, "SEVENTEEN" SINGLE, ALL INVICTA HI FI/TELSTAR, 2002/2003, ART DIRECTION: MAT MAIT-LAND, GERARD SAINT @ BIG ACTIVE, DESIGN: MAT MAITLAND @ BIG ACTIVE, PHOTOS: DONALD MILNE

151 DESIGN: INGORANZ > KATJA KNOBLICH • MUSIC: VARIOUS • CD COVERS
DESIGN: TSUYOSHI HIROOKA • MUSIC: TOO DARN COOL • CD COVER, ALBUM COVER FOR LIMITED CD OF ELLA FITZGERALD'S "TOO DARN HOT " WHICH WAS RELEASED FROM ADIDAS
DESIGN: TSUYOSHI HIROOKA • MUSIC: TEENAGE OF THE YEAR • FLYER DESIGN FOR ROCK EVENT, TEENAGE OF THE YEAR

152 DESIGN: WUFF • MUSIC: IAN POOLEY • CD COVER, „SOUVENIRS", LABEL: POOLEDMUSIC/MINISTRY OF SOUND
DESIGN: TSUYOSHI KUSANO • MUSIC: KEN ISHII • CD COVER

153 DESIGN: TSUYOSHI HIROOKA • MUSIC: TOY • POSTER DESIGN FOR ROCK EVENT, TEENAGE OF THE YEAR
DESIGN: LAURENT FETIS • MUSIC: BECK • TOUR POSTER, SEA CHANGE TOUR', 2002
DESIGN: KAREN INGRAM • MUSIC: TUSSLE • CD COVER

154 DESIGN: ROCKING JELLY BEAN • MUSIC: THEE MICHELLE GUN ELEPHANT • TOUR POSTER/SHIRT, "LAST HEAVEN TOUR 2003", © 2003 BAD MUSIC CORPORATION. ALL RIGHT RESERVED.

155 DESIGN: HONEST • MUSIC: WEEN • ILLUSTRATION

156 DESIGN: FAT CAT • MUSIC: SIGUR ROS • CD COVER
DESIGN: TRANSACOUSTIC RESEARCH • MUSIC: ROUGH MIXES • EXPERIMENTAL GRAPHICS AS 7" SLEEVE BY NIKOLAUS GANSTERER, LABEL: IFTAF REC (SUB-LABEL VON TRANSACOUSTIC RESEARCH), 1999

157 DESIGN: FAT CAT • MUSIC: SIGUR ROS • CD COVER
DESIGN: PFADFINDEREI • MUSIC: ALEX AMONN • VINYL SLEEVE

158 DESIGN: THOMAS BARWICK • MUSIC: SLUTS OF TRUST • CD COVER
DESIGN: TOMOKO TSUNEDA • MUSIC: DIXIED THE EMONS • VINYL SLEEVE
DESIGN: SYRUP • MUSIC: ESCALATOR COMPILATION • CD COVER

159 DESIGN: SEB JARNOT • MUSIC: LLORCA • CD COVER, POSTER, NEWCOMER", 2001, LABEL: F COMMUNICATIONS

160 DESIGN: BÜRO DESTRUCT • MUSIC: BALDUIN • CD SLEEVE, DESIGNER: LOPETZ, CLIENT: CRIPPLED DICK HOT WAX, BERLIN, 2003WWW.BERMUDA.CH/BALDUIN

161 DESIGN: BÜRO DESTRUCT • MUSIC: BEJAZZ WINTERFESTIVAL 2004 • FLYER AND POSTER FOR JAZZ FESTIVAL, DESIGNER: MBRUNNER, CLIENT: BEJAZZ, 2003

162 DESIGN: JDK • MUSIC: WEEN • GIG POSTER, STUDIO – JAGER DI PAOLA KEMP DESIGN, BURLINGTON, VT.; CREATIVE DIRECTOR – MICHAEL JAGER; DESIGN DIRECTOR – LANCE VIOLETTE; DESIGN – TYLER STOUT, LANCE VIOLETTE; PRINTING – COLOR SHACK

163 DESIGN: JDK • MUSIC: TENACIOUS D. • GIG POSTER, STUDIO – JAGER DI PAOLA KEMP DESIGN, BURLINGTON, VT.; CREATIVE DIRECTOR – MICHAEL JAGERDESIGN DIRECTOR – BEN NILES; DESIGN – JOE PEILA, DANA SACHS; ILLUSTRATOR – TYLER STOUT; PRINTING – COLOR SHACK

164 DESIGN: UNIVERSAL EVERYTHING • MUSIC: FREEFORM • "HUMAN" LP GATEFOLD / CD JEWELCASE • "WILDCAT", EP / CD WALLET • "YOU SHOULD GET OUT MORE", 7" SINGLE, LABEL: SKAM

165 DESIGN: ZIP • MUSIC: COSMOS • PROMO
DESIGN: TORTOISE • MUSIC: TORTOISE • CD COVER

166 DESIGN: FONS HICKMANN, BARBARA BÄTTIG • MUSIC: HAUSCHKA • CD COVER, CLIENT: VOLKER BERTELMANN, STUDIO: FONS HICKMANN M23

167 DESIGN: TYLER STOUT • MUSIC: TROUBLE EVERYDAY • POSTER
DESIGN: BIG ACTIVE • MUSIC: VIOLENT DELIGHT • CD COVERS, "TRANSMISSION" ALBUM, "WISH" SINGLE, "ALL" SINGLE, ALL WEA RECORDS, 2003, ART DIRECTION & DESIGN: RICHARD ANDREWS @ BIG ACTIVE, ILLUSTRATIONS: JODY BARTON @ BIG ACTIVE

168 DESIGN: DENNIS TYFUS • MUSIC: TRUMANS WATER • SINGLE SLEEVE, MC SLEEVE, "THE ARTYCHOCK MAN", WWW.TRUMANSWA-TER.COM, LABEL: ULTRA ECZEMA, WWW.DENNISTYFUS.TK, THIS 7" SINGLE IS MADE ON 300 COPY'S, EVERY COPY INCLUDES A DIFFE-RENT HANDRAWN COVER
DESIGN: DENNIS TYFUS • MUSIC: CASSINI DIVISION • SINGLE SLEEVE, "CASSINI DIVISION", LABEL: SUBDEVIANT RECORDINGS, HTTP://BURN.AT/SUBDEVIANT, COVER MADE WITH THE "COMPU-TER HELP" OF KEVIN APETOWN
DESIGN: TYLER STOUT • MUSIC: UNWOUND • TOUR POSTER •
MUSIC: THE EX • TOUR POSTER
DESIGN: MRZ • MUSIC: MASSIMO • CD COVER, "HELLO DIRTY", LABEL: MEGO, 2002

169 DESIGN: INSECT • MUSIC: MONK & CANATELLA • CD COVER
DESIGN: RINZEN • MUSIC: BANANAGEDDON • POSTER • MUSIC: REGURGITATOR • CD COVER, "JINGLES"
DESIGN: PURY • MUSIC: GOMER • VINYL SLEEVE

170 DESIGN: MARTIN KVAMME • MUSIC: CO-STAR • CD COVER, "BROTHERS IN CRIME EP", ONLYEVER RECORDS, 2003, PHOTO: MARTE ROGNERUD

171 DESIGN: IO • MUSIC: BLACK NOISE • CD COVER, BOOK, "ROTATIO-NAL HIGH" CD, "TALK TO ME" SINGLE, LABEL: INTEGRAL MUSIC, 2003.
DESIGN: FACTOR PRODUKT • MUSIC: MOGUAI • CD COVER

172/ DESIGN: INSECT • MUSIC: SOUTHERN FLY • CD COVERS, BOOKS

172 DESIGN: TSUYOSHI HIROOKA • MUSIC: WANNA ROCK • ILLUS-TRATIONS FOR INDIE-BAND BABAMANIA'S WANNA ROCK ALBUM (ON TEICHIKU ENTERTAINMENT)

174 DESIGN: MIRKO BORSCHE • MUSIC: MUNK • VINYL SLEEVES, MORE INFOS AT WWW.GOMMA.DE
DESIGN: FAT CAT • MUSIC: VARIOUS • THE MUTTS "MISSING MY DEVIL", STROMBA "THE PINCH", MATMOS/MOTION „SPLIT #11",

175 DESIGN: JOHN WIESE • MUSIC: SISSY SPACEK • SINGLE SLEEVE
DESIGN: ICON • MUSIC: VARIOUS • CD PACKAGINGS, ALEJANDRA & AERON "SCOTCH MONSTERS", YOSHIO MACHIDA "HYPERNATU-RAL #2", AKI ONDA "PRECIOUS MOMENTS"

176/ DESIGN: IZMOJUKI • MUSIC: MTV JAPAN • ADVERTISING, MTV JAPAN "MUSIC AND MORE" / MACHINE

178/ DESIGN: FOETUS • MUSIC: FOETUS

180 DESIGN: INKSURGE • MUSIC: SANDWICH • CD COVER, BOOK, "THANKS TO THE MOON'S GRAVITATIONAL PULL", DESIGNERS: JOYCE TAI AND REX ADVINCULA (INKSURGE), PHOTOGRAPHY: RA RIVERA, MYRENE ACADEMIA, DIEGO CASTILLO - PHILIPPINE BASED BAND NAMED "SANDWICH" RELEASED THEIR FIRST INDIE ALBUM ENTITLED "THANKS TO THE MOON'S GRAVITATIONAL PULL". INKSURGE CAME UP WITH A COLLAGE REFLECTING THE BAND'S INDIVIDUAL CHARACTER, USING THEIR PERSONAL STUFF SUCH AS HAND-WRITTEN LYRICS, POLAROID PHOTOS AND THEIR FAVORITE TOYS. RA RIVERA DIRECTED THE SHOOT FOR THE COVER.
DESIGN: FONS HICKMANN • MUSIC: VARIOUS • POSTER SERIES, "ANNONYME IDYLLE", CLIENT: JOHANNESKANTOREI, STUDIO: FONS HICKMANN M23, PHOTO: BÜRO FÜR FOTOS

181 DESIGN: MARTIN KVAMME • MUSIC: MAGNET • CD COVERS, "ON YOUR SIDE", ULTIMATE DILEMMA, 2003, LIMITED EDITION DIGIPAK PRINTED IN 4 COLOR CMYK + SILVER FOLIO (BIRDS), PHOTO: MARTE ROGNERUD • "THE DAY WE LEFT TOWN EP", ULTIMATE DILEMMA, 2003, PHOTO: MARTE ROGNERUD • "LAST DAY OF SUMMER" (SINGLE), ULTIMATE DILEMMA, 2003, SPECIAL EDITION LIMITED TO ONLY 1000 NUMBERED PRESSINGS, GATEFOLD 12" SLEEVE INCORPORATING A WHEEL FEATURING ILLUSTRATION WORK AND ALSO THE LYRICS TO THE SONG WHICH CAN BE VIE-WED THROUGH A DIE-CUT ROUND WINDOW ON THE FRONT • "LAY LADY LAY" (SINGLE), ULTIMATE DILEMMA, 2004, PHOTO: HELGE KVAMME/MARTE ROGNERUD

182 DESIGN: AUTOMATIC • MUSIC: THE PRESENCE OF HUM, SCREAMING CHEETAH WEELIES • CD COVER. SCREENIN' CHEETAH WHEELIES,"BOOGIE KING" PROMOTION CD SINGLE, LABEL: VELOCETTE RECORDS, ART DIRECTION: FRANK GARGULIO • AD: 1998 MTV MUSIC AWARDS AD, LABEL: CAPITAL RECORDS, ART DIRECTION: TOMMY STEELE
DESIGN: F27 - FACTOR 27 • MUSIC: MY MORNING JACKET • POSTER
DESIGN: REGINA • MUSIC: TONE FLOW • CD COVER
DESIGN: ASTERIK • MUSIC: JOY ELECTRIC • CD COVER

183 DESIGN: KONSTRUKTION • MUSIC: THE UNIT, COPENHAVEN JAZZ • CD COVERS, FLYERS
DESIGN: QUENTARO "ANI" FUJIMOTO • MUSIC: TANIKUGU • CD COVER, "GREASE", © RISK SYSTEM RECORDED THINGS JPN. 2003
DESIGN: PFADFINDEREI • MUSIC: BINDEMITTEL • CD COVER

184 DESIGN: STUDIO 1800 • MUSIC: THE KAMIKAZE HEARTS, NAKA-TOMI PLAZA • POSTERS, DESIGN: ROGER BOVA
DESIGN: JDK • MUSIC: J. J. CALE • POSTER, STUDIO – JAGER DI PAOLA KEMP DESIGN, BURLINGTON, VT.; CREATIVE DIRECTOR – MICHAEL JAGER; DESIGN DIRECTOR – MALCOLM BUICK; DESIGN – MALCOLM BUICK; PRINTING – COLOR SHACK

185 DESIGN: SLANG INTERNATIONAL • MUSIC: VARIOUS • GIG POSTERS: "ERIN", 1999 • "THE BOTTOM OF THE HILL CONCERT", 1999 • "EAR AND EYE CONTROL", 1998

186 DESIGN: IO • MUSIC: ISOLATION YEARS • CD COVERS, "FROSTED MINDS" E.P., "IT'S GOLDEN" ALBUM, NONS/MNW RECORDS 2003.
DESIGN: TOMOKO TSUNEDA • MUSIC: DIXIED THE EMONS • CD COVER

187 DESIGN: JONAS BANKER • MUSIC: KRISTOFER ÅSTRÖM • CD COVERS

188/ DESIGN: A.LORENZ • MUSIC: MAXIMILIAN HECKER • "INFINITE LOVE SONGS", 2001.08, CD DIGIPAK AND DLP SLEEVE, ILLUSTRATION: PAINTING BY LIISA LOUNILA, KITTY-YO INT., BERLIN 2001, KY01053CD/DLP • "POLYESTER", 2001.06, DM DIGIPAK AND 7" SLEEVE, ILLUSTRATION: PAINTING BY LIISA LOUNILA, KITTY-YO INT., BERLIN 2001, KY01050CDM/7"

189 DESIGN: INSECT • MUSIC: KOURNAKOVA • CD COVERS

190/ DESIGN: NICK HAVAS/JUSTIN JONES • MUSIC: AND ALSO THE TREES • CD COVERS

190 DESIGN: ALTERNATIVE TENTACLES • MUSIC: THE FLAMING STARS • CD COVERS

192 DESIGN: DISCODOENER • MUSIC: JOY DENALANE, FREUNDES-KREIS • CD COVERS

193 DESIGN: ZION • MUSIC: HOME SWEET HOUSE COMPILATION • CD COVER
DESIGN: METHANE • MUSIC: STEREOLAB • GIG POSTER

194 DESIGN: ENLIGHTMENT • MUSIC: VARIOUS (FROZEN HAWAII, TRIBUTE TO JOAO GIRBERT, TSUKI NO WA, THE WEDDING PROJECT) • CD COVERS

195 DESIGN: VICTORIA COLLIER • MUSIC: MOJAVE 3 • CD COVER

196 DESIGN: JAN LANKISCH • MUSIC: CASIOTONE FOR THE PAINFULLY ALONE • CD COVER, "TWINKLE ECHO", LABEL: TOMLAB, 200, PAIN-TING BY HEIDI ANDERSON, PITHYTIRB@YAHOO.COM
DESIGN: FJD • MUSIC: THE RETURNING SUN, DOGGY STYLE, A.D.M., CALM • CD COVERS: THE RETURNING SUN/VARIOUS ARTISTS, LABEL: LASTRUM • DOGGGYSTYLE/REGEMIDORI, LABEL: VICTOR ENTERTAINMENT • CALM FEATURING MOONAGE ELECTRIC ENSEMBLE/ANCIENT FUTURE, LABEL: LASTRUM • ACOUSTIC DUB MESSENGERS/BEST&REMIXES, LABEL: RIGHT TEMPO
DESIGN: HONEST • MUSIC: ZEMOG • CD COVER
DESIGN: LAURA VARSKY • MUSIC: LA ZURDA • CD COVER
DESIGN: INTERSTELLAR • MUSIC: GONE BALD • CD COVER

197 DESIGN: FJD • MUSIC: VARIOUS • CD COVERS, POSTERS • STOMACH OF GYPSYS/DOG DAY AFTERNOON, LABEL: LASTRUM • LOVERS ROCK (LIVE EVENT)AT 2001.8.19 LIQUID ROOM • GOLF/THE GIFT, LABEL: A LIGHTS

198 DESIGN: INSECT • MUSIC: HOUSE OF WAX, JACK PLANCK • CD COVERS

199 DESIGN: 2 YANG • MUSIC: G-FREAK FACTORY / NORTHERN LIGHT TRIBE • LABEL: TOSHIBA EMI • MUSIC: VARIOUS ARTISTS / BLUE FRAME DUB • LABEL: SF RECORDINGS • CD COVERS

200/ DESIGN: STEPHAN DOITSCHINOFF • MUSIC: SAVES THE DAY • CD COVER, BOOK, "IN REVERIE", "ANYWHERE WITH YOU", LABEL: DREAMWORKS RECORDS

202/ DESIGN: TOMOKO TSUNEDA • MUSIC: ACO, DIXIED THE EMONS • CD COVERS, STICKER, VIDEO PACKAGING

204/ DESIGN: EH? > EHQUESTIONMARK • MUSIC: VARIOUS • VINYL SLEEVES, LEX RECORDS • LEX RECORDS 001 EPSLEEVE "LEX GENERIC HOUSE SLEEVE" • LEX RECORDS 002 LPSLEEVE "LEX COMPILATION SLEEVE" • LEX RECORDS 003 EP SLEEVE "MANNEQUIN HAND TRAPDOOR I REMINDER" • LEX RECORDS 006 LPSLEEVE "SEED TO SUN" • LEX RECORDS 023 EPSLEEVE "WINTER'S GOING" • LEX RECORDS 024 LP INNER "ASIDE OF INNER SLEEVE", WWW.LEXRECORDS.COM

206 DESIGN: NITRADA • MUSIC: PILOT BALLOON • CD COVER
DESIGN: REGINA • MUSIC: KAOSPILOT • CD COVER, AD

207 DESIGN: KATSUMI YOKOTA • MUSIC: SO • CD COVER
DESIGN: SLANG INTERNATIONAL • MUSIC: SHOCKOUT • VINYL SLEEVE, SHOCKOUT, 12" RECORD COVER, CLIENT: SHOCKOUT, LOCATION: OAKLAND, 2003

208 DESIGN: EH? > EHQUESTIONMARK • MUSIC: BOOM BIP • VINYL SLEEVES, LEX RECORDS 014, EP SLEEVE "FROM LEFT TO RIGHT" • LEX RECORDS 020, EP SLEEVE "MORNING AND A DAY", WWW.LEX-RECORDS.COM

209 DESIGN: EH? > EHQUESTIONMARK • MUSIC: DANGER MOUSE & JEMINI • VINYL SLEEVES: LEX RECORDS 010 LPOUTER "GHETTO POP LIFE", LEX RECORDS 022 CDWALLET "TWENTY SIX INCH", WWW.LEXRECORDS.COM

210 DESIGN: FRANÇOIS CHALET • MUSIC: VARIOUS • CD COVERS, DOMIZIL 17 + 18, LABEL DOMIZIL, WWW.DOMIZIL.CH

211 DESIGN: HIDEKI INABA • MUSIC: TNW • CD BOOK: RE:MOVEMENT, 2001, CLIENT: ELECTRIC SAL/DAIICHI KOSHO CO.,LTD.
DESIGN: NITRADA • MUSIC: NITRADA • SINGLE SLEEVE
DESIGN: BOWLING CLUB • MUSIC: IDEI LAHESNA • VINYL SLEEVE

212 DESIGN: TSUYOSHI KUSANO • MUSIC: 5RB • CD COVERS
DESIGN: F27 - FACTOR 27 • MUSIC: SPOON • GIG POSTERS

213 DESIGN: LESSRAIN • MUSIC: MODIFIED TOY ORCHESTRA • SINGLE SLEEVE, LABEL: WARM CIRCUIT/MTO

214 DESIGN: RUNE MORTENSEN • MUSIC: MARTIN HORNTVETH, PAAL NILSSEN-LOVE/HÅKON KORNSTAD • CD COVERS, MARTIN HORN-TVETH "SKULL EP", LABEL: SMALLTOWN SUPERSOUND, 2003 • PAAL NILSSEN-LOVE / HAAKON KORNSTAD "SCHLINGER", LABEL: SMALLTOWN SUPERSOUND, 2003

215 DESIGN: ROBERT SAMSONOWITZ • MUSIC: KEVLAR • VINYL SLEEVE, "LET ME WORRY SOME MORE", LABEL: CHALKSOUNDS RECORDS, 2002
DESIGN: QUENTARO "ANI" FUJIMOTO • MUSIC: SUNSHOWER, FORTUNATE 1MARK, MONKEY TURN • CD COVERS, "SUNSHOWER REMIXES FINALIZED", © FAR EAST RECORDING • "FORTUNATE 1MARK", © FAR EAST RECORDING • "MONKEYTURN", © FAR EAST RECORDING
DESIGN: NOBODY • MUSIC: SING LIKE TALKING • CD COVERS, "BORDERLAND/THE LOVE WE MAKE/IN THE RHYTHM", "HELLO"
DESIGN: HONEST • MUSIC: ASTRALWERKS COMPILATION • CD COVER

216 DESIGN: ZIP • MUSIC: FUEL • VINYL SLEEVES

217 DESIGN: ZIP • MUSIC: LAZY GRACE • VINYL SLEEVES

218 DESIGN: ZIP • MUSIC: GRANDADBOB • CD COVERS

219 DESIGN: KLON • MUSIC: MARVELLOUS • CD COVER

220 DESIGN: SWEDEN • MUSIC: DR. KOSMOS • CD COVER, "DOKTOR KOSMOS" CD COVER, LABEL: NONS RECORDS, 2000, PHOTO BY: LOUISE BILLGERT
DESIGN: MIRKO BORSCHE • MUSIC: LEROY HANG HOFER • CD BOOK, MORE INFOS AT WWW.GOMMA.DE

220 DESIGN: RED • MUSIC: QUANTIC • VINYL SLEEVE

221 DESIGN: CARLOS SEGURA • MUSIC: VARIOUS • COMICS

222 DESIGN: BIG ACTIVE • MUSIC: A, ALOUD • CD COVERS: A "HI-FI SERIOUS" ALBUM, "STARBUCKS" SINGLE, "SOMETHIN'S GOING ON" SINGLE, "GOOD TIMES" SINGLE, ALL LONDON RECORDS, 2002/2003, ART DIRECTION & DESIGN: MAT MAITLAND @ BIG ACTIVE, ILLUSTRATIONS: DAVID FOLDVARI @ BIG ACTIVE • ALOUD "ALOUD" ALBUM, "BOB O'LEAN" SINGLE, "3'S UP" E.P., ALL MINI-STRY RECORDINGS., 2003/2004, ART DIRECTION & DESIGN: RICHARD ANDREWS @ BIG ACTIVE, ILLUSTRATIONS: SHIV @ BIG ACTIVE

223 DESIGN: SWEDEN • MUSIC: ODD JOB, KOMEDA • CD COVERS, ODDJOB "KOYO", KOMEDA "KOKOMEMEDADA"
DESIGN: DAN ABBOTT • MUSIC: ON TRIAL • CD COVER, LABEL: MOLTEN, 2002

224 DESIGN: KIM HIORTHØY • MUSIC: MIDNIGHT DRUMMER • VINYL SLEEVE, MIDNIGHT DRUMMER: CANNIBAL CITY, TO BE RELEASED, , LABEL: SMALLTOWN SUPERSOUND, LATE 2004.
DESIGN: DISCODOENER • MUSIC: MR.X & MR.Y • CD COVER
DESIGN: FACTOR PRODUKT • MUSIC: BOB DYLAN, DAVID MORALES • CD COVER, FLYER
DESIGN: NATIONAL FOREST • MUSIC: AL GREEN • CD COVER, LABEL: EMI
DESIGN: BÜRO DESTRUCT • MUSIC: ALPHATRONIC • CD SLEEVE, DESIGNER: H1REBER, CLIENT: INZEC RECORDS, 2003

225 DESIGN: TYLER STOUT • MUSIC: EX-BEST FRIEND, LES SAVY FAV, DEATH CAB FOR CUTIE • GIG POSTERS
DESIGN: SUPERLOW • MUSIC: BLACK LOW • POSTER
DESIGN: NATIONAL FOREST • MUSIC: UBIQUITY • POSTER

226 DESIGN: MARTIN KVAMME • MUSIC: TOMAHAWK, MELVINS • GIG POSTER, TRIBUTE, SANDNES, NORWAY, 3. JULY 2003

227 DESIGN: NONFORMAT • MUSIC: CONNECTORS • VINYL SLEEVES, CD COVERS, BARRY 7'S CONNECTORS + BARRY 7'S CONNECTORS 2, PACKAGING FOR 60S/70S LIBRARY MUSIC COMPILATION CHO-SEN BY ADD N TO (X) MEMBER BARRY 7, 2001
DESIGN: QUENTARO "ANI" FUJIMOTO • MUSIC: VARIOUS - SST • CD COVER, "BACK IN THE S.S.T. BAND!! -THE VERY BEST-", © SCI-TRON DIGITAL CONTENTS INC. 2003, © PONY CANYON INC., © SEGA CORPORATION

228 DESIGN: MARTIN KVAMME • MUSIC: FANTOMAS • GIG POSTER, ROCKEFELLER, OSLO, NORWAY, 14. JULY 2000

229 DESIGN: MARTIN KVAMME • MUSIC: TOMAHAWK • TOUR POSTER, SCANDINAVIAN TOUR, 2002

230/ DESIGN: DRAGON • MUSIC: VARIOUS • GIG/PROMOTION POSTERS, FLYER, CD COVERS

232/ DESIGN: ROCKING JELLY BEAN • MUSIC: VARIOUS • CD COVERS, ANDRE WILLIAMS / POOR MR. SANTA, 7" EP, © 1997 NORTON RECORDS • THE 5.6.7.8'S / BOMB THE ROCKS, ALBUM (CD/LP) © 2003 TIME BOMB RECORDS • GASOLINE / PERMANENTS SHAKEDOWN, ALBUM (CD), © 2003 DECKREC • THE FLAMENCO A GO GO / FULLY FED FREAKS, ALBUM (CD), © 1994 BENTEN LABEL • GUITAR WOLF / JET ROCK'N'ROLL, BOOK COVER, © BYAKUYA SHOBOU CO.,LTD.

234 DESIGN: RED • MUSIC: PISS • PICTURE DISK
DESIGN: SCUMBUCKET • MUSIC: SCUMBUCKET • CD COVER

235 DESIGN: DRAGON • MUSIC: NEW YORK TIMES - VARIOUS • CD COVER
DESIGN: IO • MUSIC: CAESARS PALACE, DUNGEN • CD COVER, VINYL SLEEVES: CAESARS PALACE, "FROM THE BUGHOUSE" SINGLE, LABEL: DOLORES RECORDINGS/VIRGIN RECORDS, 2001 • "STADSVANDRINGAR", LABEL: DOLORES RECORDINGS/VIRGIN RECORDS, 2002 • "LOVE FOR THE STREETS", LABEL: DOLORES RECORDINGS/VIRGIN RECORDS, 2002.
DESIGN: ALTERNATIVE TENTACLES • MUSIC: LARD • CD COVER
DESIGN + MUSIC: THE RAVEONETTES • CD COVER
DESIGN: FIREWATER • MUSIC: FIREWATER • CD COVER
DESIGN: MOTHER TONGUE • MUSIC: MOTHER TONGUE • CD COVER

236 DESIGN: MARTIN KVAMME • MUSIC: KAADA • PROMO POSTER, THANK YOU FOR GIVING ME YOUR VALUABLE TIME RELEASE 2003
DESIGN: AIRSIDE • MUSIC: PEOPLE IN PLANES • POSTER
DESIGN: BENJAMIN GÜDEL • MUSIC: DELIQUENT HABITS, DAVID BOWIE, TRUE COLORS • POSTER
DESIGN: 2 YANG • MUSIC: VARIOUS "JAPANESE RENAISSANCE" • POSTER

237 DESIGN: BRAINBOX • MUSIC: KAMINO • CD COVER
DESIGN: ZIP • MUSIC: STONEBRIDGE, COSMOS • CD COVERS
DESIGN: TSUYOSHI HIROOKA • MUSIC: CAPSULE, GOLDEN CHRISTMAS • CD COVERS: PROMOTION ALBUM FOR THE UNIT CALLED CAPSULE ON YAMAHA MUSIC FOUNDATION • ALBUM COVER FOR FREE CD "SELFISH"
DESIGN: K7 • MUSIC: MAS • CD COVER

238 DESIGN: TSUYOSHI KUSANO • MUSIC: VARIOUS • BOX

239 DESIGN: NONFORMAT • MUSIC: ROOT PROJECT THURSTON MOORE • CD PACKAGING, CALL FOR ENTRIES - A DAT CONTAINING ONE OF 30 ONE-MINUTE GUITAR PIECE BY SONIC YOUTH'S THURSTON MOORE WAS SENT OUT TO ONE HUNDRED ARTISTS AND MUSICIANS IN A SPECIALLY PRODUCED VACUUM CLEANER BAG. THE ARTISTS AND MUSICIANS WERE ASKED TO PRODUCE A NEW WORK INCORPORATING THE ORIGINAL PIECE IN SOME WAY. LIMITED EDITION CD PACKAGING - A CD BY A SELECTION OF THE MUSICIANS WAS PRODUCED. LIMITED EDITIONS WERE PRODUCED IN A CUSTOMISED VACUUM CLEANER BAG. 1998/1999.

240 DESIGN: AIRSIDE • MUSIC: LEMON JELLY • SINGLE PACKAGING, "SOFT", "ROLLED OATS"

241 DESIGN: DENNIS TYFUS • MUSIC: THE WOMUPS • CD PACKAGING, WWW.WOMUPS.TK, LABEL: SELF RELEASED, WWW.DENNISTYFUS.TK, WWW.JELLECRAMA.TK, WWW.ESESRECORDS.COMMAIL GRAFIKER; DENNISTYFUS@HOTMAIL.COM, ONCE THE COVER IS UNFOLT, IT'S VERY HARD TO FOLD BACK...

242 DESIGN: MANFRED ENGELMAYR • MUSIC: BULBUL • CD PACKA-GING IRON, WWW.BULBUL.AT, LABEL: TROST, WWW.TROST.AT

243 DESIGN: MANFRED ENGELMAYR, TOM HULAN • MUSIC: BULBUL • CD PACKAGING VELO, WWW.BULBUL.AT, LABEL: TROST, WWW.TROST.AT
DESIGN: TOM HULAN • MUSIC: BULBUL • CD PACKAGING FEATHER "WASSERTURM FAVORITEN", WWW.BULBUL.AT, LABEL: RASPUTIN RECORDS HURENSCHAEDL, WWW.RASPRECHS.COM

244/ DESIGN: CHARHIZMA / D+ • MUSIC: CHARHIZMA COMPILATION PROJECT „PLATTE" • SPECIAL VINYL PACKAGING (WITH FAKE PIC-TURE DISKS), LABEL: CHARHIZMA & JIMMY DRAHT, WWW.CHARHIZMA.COM/PLATTE/, WWW.JIMMY-DRAHT.DE CARDBOARD GRAPHIC: OLIVER GRAJEWSKI, MARKUS HUBER, CX HUTH, BATIA KOLTON, JAN KRUSE, LÉO, GERDA RAIDT, BILLY ROISZ, SABINE TIMM, JIM AVIGNONSOUND: DIEB13, DRIK M., I-SOUND, MARTIN NG, OTOMO YOSHIHIDE

246/ DESIGN: CHARHIZMA / D+ • MUSIC: ORCHESTER 33 1/3 • SPECIAL CD PACKAGING (OUT OF OLD RECORDS), LABEL: CHARHIZMA, WWW.CHARHIZMA.COM/33/INDEX.HTML

246 DESIGN: JARED CONNOR • MUSIC: MODEST MOUSE • SPECIAL FLYER/ POSTER, 2 COLOR SILKSCREEN 10"X6.5", ON CHIPBOARD WITH MOUSE TRAPS IN PLASTIC BAG

247 DESIGN: F27 - FACTOR 27 • MUSIC: THE FLAMING LIPS • SPECIAL FLYER/ POSTER

248 DESIGN: MONGREL • MUSIC: BIKINI WAX • POSTER

249 DESIGN: NONFORMAT • MUSIC: THE CHAP • POSTER, VINYL SLEEVE, CD COVER: "THE HORSE", PRINTED IN FLUORESCENT PINK AND SILVER INK. 2003

250 DESIGN: GODSPEED YOU BLACK EMPEROR • MUSIC: GODSPEED YOU BLACK EMPEROR • CD COVER
DESIGN: NITRADA • MUSIC: STATE RIVER WIDENING • SINGLE SLEEVE
DESIGN: NITRADA • MUSIC: • SINGLE SLEEVE

251 DESIGN: AGUST ÆEVAR GUNNARSSON • MUSIC: SIGUR ROS • CD COVER
DESIGN: STRUGGLE • MUSIC: ELECTRO-ROLLER-BOOGIE-TECHNO-DISCO • VINYL SLEEVE, "XYLOPHONE JONES" GENERIC SLEEVE, LABEL: XYLOPHONE JONES, ILLUSTRATION: CODY HUDSON

252 DESIGN: ZION • MUSIC: THOMAS RUSIAK • CD COVER, BOOK

253 DESIGN: STUDIO 1800 • MUSIC: THE BRIAN JONESTOWN MASSACRE • POSTER, DESIGN: CHRIS RUBINO

254 DESIGN: INSECT • MUSIC: SAVILE ROBOTS • VINYL SLEEVE
DESIGN: SUPERLOW • MUSIC: THORNS • CD COVER
DESIGN: SURFACE • MUSIC: SHANTEL • CD COVER, "BUCOVINA CLUB"

255 DESIGN: HEADS OF STATE • MUSIC: BONNIE PRINCE BILLY • GIG POSTER
DESIGN: SHRINE • MUSIC: FLORA REED • GIG POSTER
DESIGN: MIKE KING • MUSIC: NICK CAVE, BEN HARPER • GIG POSTERS
DESIGN: ROCKING JELLY BEAN • MUSIC: JACKIE AND THE CEDRICS • GIG POSTER

256 DESIGN: ASTERIK • MUSIC: VARIOUS • TOUR POSTER

257 DESIGN: ZION • MUSIC: THOMAS RUSIAK • CD COVER

258/ DESIGN: MARTIN KVAMME • MUSIC: TOMAHAWK • CD COVER, "MIT GAS", IPECAC RECORDINGS, 2003, PRINTED: BLACK, BRONZE METALLIC FOLIO, DESIGN: MARTIN KVAMME AND MIKE PATTON

260/ DESIGN: USUGROW • MUSIC: EVIL C, ABNORMALS, BEAST TEAST, SHADOWSFALL, VARIOUS • CD COVERS, GIG POSTERS: EVIL.C / BUDDHIST SONG (DEMO FRONT COVER), EVIL.C / TARANTISM (FRONT COVER), ABNORMALS / HATRED (FRONT COVER), ABNOR-MALS / HATRED (POSTER), BEAST FEAST 2002, SHADOWS FALL / CRUSHING BELIAL, DESSERT / WORLD OF FANTASY, PULLING TEETH / PAIN AND PATIENCE, PINHOLE+21 / CANDATA, © COPY-RIGHT USUGROW

262/ DESIGN: SUPERLOW • MUSIC: SATYRICON • VINYL SLEEVE, LABELS POSTER

264/ DESIGN: FAT CAT • MUSIC: VARIOUS • CD COVERS: SET FIRE TO FLAMES "SINGS REIGN REBUILDER" & TELEGRAPHS IN NEGATIVE", MAX RICHTER "THE BLUE NOTEBOOKS", SYLVAIN CHAUVEAU " UN AUTRE DECEMBRE"

266 DESIGN: INSECT • MUSIC: ARCHIVE • CD COVERS

267 DESIGN: CARLOS SEGURA • MUSIC: VARIOUS • CD COVERS

268/ DESIGN: DIRK RUDOLPH • MUSIC: COVENANT, DE/VISION • CD

269 COVERS, BOOKS

270 DESIGN: DIRK RUDOLPH • MUSIC: IN EXTREMO, ILSE DELANGE • CD COVERS, BOOKS

271 DESIGN: DIRK RUDOLPH • MUSIC: APOCALYPTICA, RAMMSTEIN • CD COVERS, BOOKS

272 DESIGN: DIRK RUDOLPH • MUSIC: IN EXTREMO • CD COVERS, BOOKS

273 DESIGN: DIRK RUDOLPH • MUSIC: PIA LUND • CD COVERS, BOOKS

274 DESIGN: STYLOROUGE • MUSIC: HALO • CD COVER

275 DESIGN: BIG ACTIVE • MUSIC: SYNTAX • CD PACKAGING, "MECCANO MIND" PROMO, LABEL: ILLUSTRIOUS/SONY, 2004, ART DIRECTION: MAT MAITLAND, GERARD SAINT @ BIG ACTIVE, PRODUCTION: DANIEL MASON (SOMETHING ELSE)

276 DESIGN: BLIND RESEARCH • MUSIC: THOROFON • VINYL SLEEVES, MC COVER, CD COVER, "FINAL MOVEMENT" VINYL, 2001, "BLOODHEAT EDITION 10_", 2003, LABEL: UMB/RITALIN AKTIF • "WE KICKED THE AUDIENCE" C90, 2001, LABEL: UMB/RITALIN AKTIF • "THIS SUMMER SUICIDE" CD, 2003, LABEL: L.WHITE REC.

277 DESIGN: DIRK RUDOLPH • MUSIC: RAMMSTEIN • DVD COVER
278/ DESIGN: DIRK RUDOLPH • MUSIC: BLACKMAIL • CD COVERS

280 DESIGN: F27 - FACTOR 27 • MUSIC: BUZZCOCKS • GIG POSTER
DESIGN: JARED CONNOR • MUSIC: JON SPENCER BLUES EXPLOSION • GIG POSTER, 3 COLOR OFFSET 11"X17", EDITION OF 250
DESIGN: CHUCK LOOSE • MUSIC: SLAYER • GIG POSTER

281 DESIGN: JARED CONNOR • MUSIC: SOCIAL DISTORTION • GIG POSTER, 2 COLOR SILKSCREEN 24"X36", EDITION OF 75
DESIGN: ZION • MUSIC: THE FAINT, RADIO 4 • GIG POSTER
DESIGN: KLANGKRIEG • MUSIC: AMERICAN BREAKBEAT COMPILATION • CD COVERS, DESIGN: HOLLIE & FLOCKEY / GRACO (WWW.GRACO-BERLIN.DE)

282/ DESIGN: MARTIN KVAMME • MUSIC: FANTOMAS • CD COVER, BOOK "DELÌRIUM CÒRDIA", IPECAC RECORDINGS, 2004, PRINTED: 4 COLOR CMYK, SILVER PANTONE, UV COATING GLOSS, UV COATING MATTE; SMOKEN BLACK JEWELCASE. DESIGN: MARTIN KVAMME AND MIKE PATTON, PHOTO: MAX AGUILERA HELLWEG

284 DESIGN: MARTIN KVAMME • MUSIC: GLUECIFER • CD COVER, "AUTOMATIC THRILL", SONY/EPIC/SPV, 2004, PRINTED SILVER PANTONE ON BLACK., GLOSS UV COATING MOTIVES PRINTED ON TOP. PHOTO: OBSERVATORIET

285 DESIGN: ROBERT SAMSONOWITZ • MUSIC: THE NEW MESS • CD COVER, "THE NEW MESS", LABEL: KASUAL RECORDINGS, 2003

286/ DESIGN: SUPERLOW • MUSIC: THORNS • CD COVER

288 DESIGN: DIRK RUDOLPH • MUSIC: DIE TOTEN HOSEN • CD COVERS

289 DESIGN: MARTIN KVAMME • MUSIC: FANTOMAS • CD COVER, PROMO POSTER, "THE DIRECTOR'S CUT", IPECAC RECORDINGS, 2001, PRINTED ON GOLD FOLIO PAPER. DESIGN: MARTIN KVAMME AND MIKE PATTON, PHOTO: KAI MYHRE

290 DESIGN: AKIRA SASAKI • MUSIC: JIM O'ROURKE & MIRROR • TOUR POSTER
DESIGN: MIKE KING • MUSIC: SLEATER KINNEY • GIG POSTER

291 DESIGN: KING MINI • MUSIC: THE MAGNOLIAS, SCENE CREAMERS • GIG POSTERS
DESIGN: HEADS OF STATE • MUSIC: THE TROUBLE WITH SWEENEY • GIG POSTER
DESIGN: MARTIN KVAMME • MUSIC: WEEN • GIG POSTER, ROCKEFELLER, OSLO, NORWAY, 28. NOVEMBER 2003

DESIGN: JDK • MUSIC: YO LA TENGO • GIG POSTER, STUDIO – JAGER DI PAOLA KEMP DESIGN, BURLINGTON, VT.; CREATIVE DIRECTOR – MICHAEL JAGER; DESIGN DIRECTOR – MALCOLM BUICK; DESIGN – DENIS KEGLER; PRINTING – COLOR SHACK
DESIGN: STUDIO 1800 • MUSIC: ...WITH THE GOODS • GIG POSTER, DESIGN: ROGER BOVA

292/ DESIGN: DIRK BONSMA • MUSIC: VARIOUS • GIG POSTERS

294 DESIGN: SMALL STAKES • MUSIC: ALKALINE TRIO, Q NOT AN U • GIG POSTERS
DESIGN: HEADS OF STATE • MUSIC: KARATE • GIG POSTER
DESIGN: MIKE KING • MUSIC: INTERPOL • GIG POSTER
DESIGN: F27 - FACTOR 27 • MUSIC: SPOON • GIG POSTER

295 DESIGN: HEADS OF STATE • MUSIC: ELLIOTT, SPUTNIK, OWLS • GIG POSTERS
DESIGN: F27 - FACTOR 27 • MUSIC: DOVES • GIG POSTER
DESIGN: MARTIN KVAMME • MUSIC: FANTOMAS • PROMO POSTER. DELÌRIUM CÒRDIA RELEASE 2004

296 DESIGN: BRIAN EWING • MUSIC: DASHBOARD CONFESSIONAL • GIG POSTER

297 DESIGN: BRIAN EWING • MUSIC: MELVINS ISIS • GIG POSTER

298 DESIGN: EMEK • MUSIC: NINE INCH NAILS, TOOL, ABA SHANTI I, CESARIA EVORA • GIG POSTERS
DESIGN: 2YANG • MUSIC: ABA SHANTI-I • GIG POSTER

299 DESIGN: EMEK • MUSIC: QUEENS OF THE STONEAGE • GIG POSTER

300 DESIGN: JUSTIN HAMPTON • MUSIC: MELVIN, TOMAHAWK • GIG POSTER
DESIGN: MIKE KING • MUSIC: RESIDENTS • GIG POSTER

301 DESIGN: JUSTIN HAMPTON • MUSIC: WHITE STRIPES • GIG POSTER

302 DESIGN: BRIAN EWING • MUSIC: HELLACOPTERS • GIG POSTER

303 DESIGN: BRIAN EWING • MUSIC: THE FIRE THEFT • GIG POSTER

304 DESIGN: BRIAN EWING • MUSIC: BILLY IDOL, DIVISION OF LAURA LEE, BRAND NEW, DEATH CAB FOR CUTIE, THE LOCUST, ERASE, YEAH YEAH YEAH'S • GIG POSTER

305 DESIGN: BRIAN EWING • MUSIC: MELVINS, NO KNIFE, BLOOD BROTHERS, PRETTY GIRLS MAKE GRAVE, ELLIOT SMITH, THE MARS VOLTA, JETS TO BRAZIL • GIG POSTER

306 DESIGN: EMEK • MUSIC: WHITE STRIPES • GIG POSTER

307 DESIGN: EMEK • MUSIC: YEAH YEAH YEAH'S • GIG POSTER
DESIGN: HEADS OF STATE • MUSIC: MODEST MOUSE • GIG POSTER
DESIGN: 33RPM • MUSIC: LE TIGRE • GIG POSTER
DESIGN: TSUYOSHI HIROOKA • MUSIC: WANNA ROCK • GIG POSTER, VISUALS FOR INDIE-BAND BABAMANIA'S WANNA ROCK ALBUM (ON TEICHIKU ENTERTAINMENT)
DESIGN: METHANE • MUSIC: THE FAGS • GIG POSTER
DESIGN: 33RPM • MUSIC: MIRAH • GIG POSTER
DESIGN: ASTERIK • MUSIC: PAPA ROACH • GIG POSTER

308 DESIGN: RUNE MORTENSEN • MUSIC: JIM STÄRK, MAGNET • POSTER, 2004
DESIGN: DYHR.HAGEN • MUSIC: SWAN LEE • CD DIGIPACK
DESIGN: VICTORIA COLLIER • MUSIC: NEIL HALSTEAD • CD COVER

309 DESIGN: JDK • MUSIC: BETH ORTON • POSTER, STUDIO – JAGER DI PAOLA KEMP DESIGN, BURLINGTON, VT.; CREATIVE DIRECTOR – MICHAEL JAGER; DESIGN DIRECTOR – MALCOLM BUICK; DESIGN – RUBY LEE; PRINTING – COLOR SHACK

310 DESIGN: BURNFIELD • MUSIC: PLUXUS • VINYL SLEEVE, CD COVER, "EUROPEAN ONION", 2002

311 DESIGN: DAVE GINK • MUSIC: THE VINES • GIG POSTER

312 DESIGN: STUDIO 1800 • MUSIC: THE BOGGS • TOUR POSTERS, ILLUSTRATION: CHRIS RUBINO
DESIGN: SHRINE • MUSIC: MEDESKI • POSTER
DESIGN: MARTIN KVAMME • MUSIC: LAMB • GIG POSTER, ROCKEFELLER, OSLO, NORWAY, 27. NOVEMBER 2002
DESIGN: MIKE KING • MUSIC: FLATSTOCK • POSTER

313 DESIGN: RUNE MORTENSEN • MUSIC: LAMBCHOP, YO LA TENGO, THURTON MOORE • GIG POSTERS, SO WHAT INDEPENDENT CLUB, 1999 – 2001
DESIGN: HYDRAFUSE • MUSIC: WEEZER • TOUR POSTER
DESIGN: NATIONAL FOREST • MUSIC: UBIQUITY • TOUR POSTER

314 DESIGN: 33RPM • MUSIC: PEDRO, THE LION • GIG POSTER
DESIGN: KING MINI • MUSIC: BUILT TO SPILL, JOHNNY MARR, SPIRITUALIZED • GIG POSTERS

315 DESIGN: 33RPM • MUSIC: THE TURN-ONS • GIG POSTER
DESIGN: KING MINI • MUSIC: PEDRO, THE LION, THE LONESOME ORGANIST, THERMALS • GIG POSTERS

316 DESIGN: 33RPM • MUSIC: FCS NORTH • GIG POSTER
DESIGN: JDK • MUSIC: ELLIOT SMITH • GIG POSTER, STUDIO – JAGER DI PAOLA KEMP DESIGN, BURLINGTON, VT.; CREATIVE DIRECTOR – MICHAEL JAGER; DESIGN DIRECTOR – RICHARD CURREN; DESIGN – RICHARD CURREN, PRINTING – COLOR SHACK
DESIGN: MIKE KING • MUSIC: SUBSTRATE, WIRE, ARIAS • GIG POSTERS

317 DESIGN: 33RPM • MUSIC: DISMEMBERMENT PLAN, DREW VICTOR • GIG POSTERS
DESIGN: MIKE KING • MUSIC: RYKO • GIG POSTER

318 DESIGN: SMALL STAKES • MUSIC: BEN KWELLER, DEATH CAB FOR CUTIE, THE AMERICAN ANALOG SET, LES SAVY FAV, AGAINST ME! • GIG POSTERS

319 DESIGN: SMALL STAKES • MUSIC: PEDRO, THE LION, SUGARCULT, DEATH CAB FOR CUTIE, WHY?, FLATSTOCK • GIG POSTERS

320 DESIGN: HEADS OF STATE • MUSIC: PINBACK, VARIOUS, Q AND NOT U, J. MASCIS • GIG POSTERS

321 DESIGN: HEADS OF STATE • MUSIC: CAT POWER, AMERICAN ANALOG SET • GIG POSTERS
DESIGN: SMALL STAKES • MUSIC: RAINER MARIA, THE DECEMBERISTS • GIG POSTERS
DESIGN: MIKE KING • MUSIC: THE KLEZMATICS • GIG POSTER

322 DESIGN: HEADS OF STATE • MUSIC: DESAPARECIDOS, THE DILLINGER ESCAPE PLAN • GIG POSTERS

323 DESIGN: HEADS OF STATE • MUSIC: CURSIVE, HOT HOT HEAT • GIG POSTERS

324 DESIGN: SMALL STAKES • MUSIC: ROB GROW • GIG POSTER

325 DESIGN: HEADS OF STATE • MUSIC: PRETTY GIRLS MAKE GRAVE, AND THEY WILL KNOW US BY THE TRAIL OF DEATH, ERASE ERRATA • GIG POSTERS

326 DESIGN: STUDIO 1800 • MUSIC: THE RAPTURE • GIG POSTER, ILLUSTRATION: CHRIS RUBINO

327 DESIGN: HEADS OF STATE • MUSIC: BUILT TO SPILL • GIG POSTER

CONTACTS

MIKE KING
CRASHDESIGN@QWEST.NET
WWW.CRASHAMERICA.COM
75, 255, 290, 294, 300, 312, 316, 317, 321

MINUS
INFO@MINUS.DE
WWW.MINUS.DE
82, 83

MIRKO BORSCHE
INFO@GOMMA.DE
WWW.GOMMA.DE
174, 220

MONGREL
INFO@MONGRELASSOCIATES.COM
WWW.MONGRELASSOCIATES.COM
248

MONITOR POP
INFO@MONITORPOP.DE
MONITORPOP.DE, WWW.CRIPPLED.DE
24, 118

MOSS DESIGN UNIT
MD@MOSSD.COM
WWW.MOSSD.COM
98

NATIONAL FOREST
CONTACT@NATIONALFOREST.COM
WWW.NATIONALFOREST.COM
101, 224, 225, 313

NICK HAVAS/JUSTIN JONES
HTTP://HOME.FREEUK.COM/AATT/
AATT@FREEUK.COM
190, 191

NICOLAS BOURQUIN | ONLAB
NIC@ONLAB.CH
WWW.ONLAB.CH
105

NOBODY > SEISHIRO "RITO" FUJIMOTO
RITO@BEATSERVICE.COM
WWW.BEATSERVICE.COM
215

NONFORMAT
INFO@EKHORNFORSS.COM
WWW.NON-FORMAT.COM
6, 7, 9, 36, 48, 79, 98, 227, 239, 249

PFADFINDEREI
CRITZLA@PFADFINDEREI.COM
WWW.PFADFINDEREI.COM
22, 79, 94, 116, 157, 183

PLAY > PRODUCTS OF PLAY
ERIC@PLAYPUPPY.COM
WWW.PLAYPUPPY.COM
56, 57

POSITRON
DOI@THE-POSITRON.COM
WWW.THE-POSITRON.COM
20

PROPELLA
PROPELLA@PROPELLA.NET
WWW.PROPELLA.NET
142

PURY
MF@PURY.ORG
WWW.PURY.ORG
169

QUENTARO "ANI" FUJIMOTO
QUEN@NENDO.COM
WWW.NENDO.COM
46, 47, 183, 215, 227

RALPH STEINBRÜCHEL
STEINBRUCHEL@SYNCHRON.CH
WWW.SYNCHRON.CH
107, 109, 132

RED DESIGN
INFO@RED-DESIGN.CO.UK
WWW.RED-DESIGN.CO.UK
29, 53, 85, 126, 220, 234

REGINA
REPUBLICOFREGINA@HOTMAIL.COM
WWW.HANDSOME.NE.JP/~ROR/
107, 182, 206

RINZEN
THEY@RINZEN.COM
WWW.RINZEN.COM
169

ROBERT SAMSONOWITZ
RBRT@RBRT.ORG
WWW.RBRT.ORG
88, 215, 285

ROCKIN' JELLY BEAN
RJB@ROCKINJELLYBEAN.COM
WWW.ROCKINJELLYBEAN.COM
154, 232, 233, 255

RUNE MORTENSEN
POST@RUNEMORTENSEN.NO
WWW.RUNEMORTENSEN.NO
53, 60, 85, 86, 87, 98, 116, 133, 214, 308, 313

SARAH LITTASY
OFFICE@CUTTINGS.AT
WWW.CUTTINGS.AT
12, 13, 19, 148

SEB JARNOT
CONTACT@SEBJARNOT.COM
WWW.SEBJARNOT.COM
159, 179

SHRINE
SHRINEDESIGN@MINDSPRING.COM
WWW.SHRINE-DESIGN.COM
37, 146, 255, 312

SLANG INTERNATIONAL > NATHANAËL HAMON
NAT@SLANGINTERNATIONAL.ORG
WWW.SLANGINTERNATIONAL.ORG
100, 105, 185, 207

SMALL STAKES, THE > JASON MUNN
JASON@THESMALLSTAKES.COM
WWW.THESMALLSTAKES.COM
294, 318, 319, 321, 324

SO TAKAHASHI > HEADS INK
INFO@WWW.HEADSINC.COM
WWW.HEADSINC.COM
37, 45, 98

SPEZIALMATERIAL
KONTAKT@SPEZIALMATERIAL.CH
WWW.SPEZIALMATERIAL.CH
89, 102, 103, 104, 106, 108

STEPHAN DOITSCHINOFF
INFO@STEPHANDOIT.COM.BR
WWW.STEPHANDOIT.COM.BR
200, 201

STRUGGLE
BIGSTRUG@HOTMAIL.COM
WWW.STRUGGLEINC.COM
98, 126, 137, 251

STUDIO 1800
CRUBINO@STUDIO18HUNDRED.COM
WWW.STUDIO18HUNDRED.COM
184, 253, 291, 312, 326

STYLOROUGE
INFO@STYLOROUGE.CO.UK
WWW.STYLOROUGE.CO.UK
52, 56, 57, 77, 84, 274

SUPERLOW > HALVOR BODIN
HAL@SUPERLOW.COM
WWW.SUPERLOW.COM
91, 225, 254, 262, 263, 286, 287

SURFACE
INFO@SURFACE.DE
WWW.SURFACE.DE
34, 35, 75, 113, 254

SWEDEN
HELLO@SWEDENGRAPHICS.COM
WWW.SWEDENGRAPHICS.COM
143, 220, 223

SYRUP
OFFICE@SYRUPHELSINKI.COM
WWW.SYRUPHELSINKI.COM
158

THOMAS BARWICK
TOM.BARWICK@VIRGIN.NET
WWW.THOMASBARWICK.COM
158

TIMO NOVOTNY
TIMO@VIDOK.ORG
WWW.VIDOK.ORG
59

TINA FRANK
TINA@FRANK.AT
WWW.FRANK.AT
85

TOM HULAN > BLACK JUNE
INFO@BLACKJUNE.COM
WWW.BLACKJUNE.COM
243

TOMOKO TSUNEDA
TSUNE@PLUM.OCN.NE.JP
WWW12.OCN.NE.JP/~TSUNE
141, 158, 186, 202, 203

TSUYOSHI HIROOKA
HIROOKA_TSUYOSHI@YBB.NE.JP
HTTP://HIRO=KA.JPN.ORG
145,151,153,172,237,307

TSUYOSHI KUSANO
TSUYOS-K@MOMO.SO-NET.NE.JP
56, 130, 152, 212, 238

TYLER STOUT
TYLER@TSTOUT.COM
WWW.TSTOUT.COM
167, 168, 225

UNIVERSAL EVERYTHING
MATT@UNIVERSALEVERYTHING.COM
WWW.UNIVERSALEVERYTHING.COM
79, 107, 135, 164

USUGROW
USUGROW@USUGROW.COM
WWW.USUGROW.COM
260, 261

VICTORIA COLLIER
VICTORIACOLLIER@BEGGARS.COM
195, 308

WUFF DESIGN
CONTACT@WUFFDESIGN.DE
WWW.WUFFDESIGN.DE
94, 152

YACHT ASSOCIATES
INFO@YACHTASSOCIATES.COM
WWW.YACHTASSOCIATES.COM
16

ZION GRAPHICS
RICKY@ZIONGRAPHICS.COM
WWW.ZIONGRAPHICS.COM
26, 36, 49, 80, 84, 113, 193, 252, 257, 281

ZIP DESIGN
CHARLIE@ZIPDESIGN.CO.UK
WWW.ZIPDESIGN.CO.UK
17, 21, 138, 165, 216, 217, 218, 237

WE WOULD LIKE TO THANK THE FOLLOWING LABELS
FOR THEIR SUPPORT AND CONTRIBUTION:

ALTERNATIVE TENTACLES
WWW.ALTERNATIVETENTACLES.COM
190, 235

BOOGIZM
WWW.BOOGIZM.NET
134

DISKO B
WWW.DISKOB.COM
140

ENDURO
INGORANZ, KATJA KNOBLICH,...
WWW.ENDURO-DISKS.DE
141, 151

FAT CAT
SIGUR ROS/AGUST ÆEVAR GUNNARSSON
WWW.FAT-CAT.CO.UK
76, 129, 156, 157, 174, 251, 264, 265

GOMMA REC.
WW.GOMMA.DE
174, 220

G-STONE
WWW.G-STONED.COM
13

INTERSTELLAR
WWW.INTERSTELLARRECORDS.AT
196

NORMAL RECORDS
WWW.NORMAL-RECORDS.COM
135

!K7
WWW.K7.COM
40, 79, 237

KLANGKRIEG
WWW.KLANGKRIEG-PRODUKTIONEN.DE
281

KRANKY
WWW.KRANKY.NET
GODSPEED YOU BLACK EMPEROR
250

MEGO
MRZ, TINA FRANK
WWW.MEGO.AT
168

NOISOLUTION
SCUMBUCKET, MOTHER TONGUE, FIREWATER
WWW.NOISOLUTION.DE
234, 235

THRILL JOCKEY
TORTOISE, KATSUMI YOKOTA, RE-P, OVAL, SUE GARNER
WWW.THRILLJOCKEY.COM
95, 110, 129, 166, 207

SOURCE RECORDS
WWW.SOURCE-RECORDS.COM
77, 91, 132

TOMLAB
MATT PYKE, JAN LANKISCH, ICON DESIGN
WWW.TOMLAB.DE
79, 91, 131, 135, 196

TRANSACOUSTIC RESEARCH
WWW.TRANSACOUSTIC-RESEARCH.COM
38, 136, 137, 140, 156

2ND REC.
NITRADA, D. SCHELLNEGGER, JOHAN & JETHRO
WWW.2NDREC.COM
69, 135, 138, 206, 211, 250

SONIC - VISUALS FOR MUSIC

Edited by Robert Klanten, Hendrik Hellige, Tom Hulan

Layout by Hendrik Hellige, Tom Hulan

Digital photos taken with Canon G5 courtesy of
Canon Deutschland GmbH. Special thanks to Bettina Steeger.
Technical support by Karl-Heinz Piur,
Canon Deutschland GmbH

Cover photo by Piet Truhlar, Styling by Suni Hoffmann,
Model: Inga @ Seeds, Clothes: Uli Dziallas & Orlando,
Studio: Haedler + Haedler

Printed by Artes Graficas Palermo, Madrid. Made in Europe.
2nd printing, 2005

Published by Die Gestalten Verlag, Berlin · London, 2004
ISBN 3-89955-040-4

For more information please check:
www.die-gestalten.de